MANIFEST DESTINY 2.0

Postwestern Horizons

MANIFEST DESTINY 2.0

GENRE TROUBLE IN GAME WORLDS

Sara Humphreys

UNIVERSITY OF NEBRASKA PRESS   LINCOLN

An earlier version of chapter 1 was published as
"Rejuvenating 'Eternal Inequality' on the Digital
Frontiers of *Red Dead Redemption*," *Western
American Literature* 47, no. 2 (2012): 200–215.

Library of Congress Cataloging-in-Publication Data
Names: Humphreys, Sara, author.
Title: Manifest destiny 2.0: genre trouble
in game worlds / Sara Humphreys.
Description: Lincoln: University of Nebraska
Press, 2021. | Series: Postwestern horizons |
Includes bibliographical references and index.
Identifiers: LCCN 2020011782
ISBN 9780803268470 (hardback)
ISBN 9781496224217 (paperback)
ISBN 9781496224781 (epub)
ISBN 9781496224798 (mobi)
ISBN 9781496224804 (pdf)
Subjects: LCSH: Western stories in video games.
| Noir fiction in video games. | Narration in
video games. | Video games—Literary themes,
motives. | Influence (Literary, artistic, etc.)
Classification: LCC GV1469.34.W47
H85 2021 | DDC 794.8—dc23
LC record available at https://lccn.loc.gov/2020011782

Set in Lyon by Laura Buis.
Designed by N. Putens.

CONTENTS

ILLUSTRATIONS

ACKNOWLEDGMENTS

This book took six years to complete, which means I may have forgotten some of the colleagues, friends, and family who helped me to complete it. To those I do not mention, thank you. Of course, I need to thank my son, who started it all by asking to play *Red Dead Redemption*. Actually, I think he begged, because he was only fourteen at the time, but I relented as long as I could play with him. I can distinctly remember peals of laughter as I tried to master the controls (I wasn't a console gamer at the time), but I did it, and here we are. I also need to thank my husband for supporting me wholeheartedly. He did more than his share around the house—I owe him six years of dishes, laundry, vet visits, chauffeuring kids, and more. Oh yes, he was also loving and supportive. Then there were the myriad of colleagues, Erin Kelly, Zailig Pollock, Michael Morse, Kelly McGuire, Sally Chivers, and Michael Epp, just to name a few, who offered encouragement and suggestions. There were also many undergraduate students at Trent University and the University of Victoria who wrote papers on the Western that helped me to remember my audience and purpose for the project. My deepest thanks to all of you.

I particularly need to thank my supervisor, now friend and colleague, Victoria Lamont, for her sage advice and patience as she read chapters and commented. I need to thank Christine Bold, who supported this project through her work and also collegial generosity. She is an unparalleled scholar and warm facilitator.

Finally, I would also like to thank the Western Literature Association for allowing me to test chapters at its wild and wonderful conferences; the University of Nebraska Press (and its intrepid editorial team) for their guidance and patience; the reviewers, who took the time to make extensive, helpful comments; and the Indigenous Literary Studies Association and the People and the Text (peopleandthetext.ca) for sharing a great deal of wisdom regarding how to treat Indigenous literatures with respect.

MANIFEST DESTINY 2.0

Introduction

A genre lives in the present but always remembers its past, its beginning.
—Mikhail Bakhtin, *Problems of Dostoevsky's Poetics*

The audience knows what to expect and it's all they are prepared to believe in.
—Tom Stoppard, *Rosencrantz and Guildenstern Are Dead*

The implications of creating game worlds from durable literary genres is the key focus of this book.[1] Durable literary genres direct the procedural rhetoric of a game world, including gameplay, rewards, collectibles, and any other rule-based representations or interactions. If procedurality refers to "the practice of encapsulating specific real-world behaviors into programmatic representations," then durable literary genres have a role to play in how those representations operate.[2] Not only do durable literary genres mediate the procedural rhetoric in a game world, their conventions tend to control the narrative as a whole. By "durable" I mean genres that have become entrenched across the Western cultural field, shaping how genders, races, classes, and even nations are perceived. Literary genres are not born in a vacuum but originate from powerful stories that have shaped how we think, fantasize, and behave. To prove my point, I track how the Western and Hollywood noir, particularly the hard-boiled variety, operate in two popular game worlds: *Red Dead Redemption* (2010) and *L.A. Noire* (2011).[3]

Durable literary genres supply an expressive cultural engine, so to speak, for game worlds to produce a coherent universe for players to situate themselves within. Game worlds are not wholly separate from "textual, visual, and plastic representation" but are different because "procedural systems like computer software actually represent process with process. This is where the particular power of procedural authorship lies, in its native ability to depict processes."[4] That is, while print, film, and even forms of digital audio broadcasting can *attempt* to represent genders, sexualities, race, class, objects, and so forth, game worlds "represent process with process." These processes are generated through computational procedures, but those procedures are not produced out of thin air. They are written by people, who are trained through mass culture to value certain stories and genres over others. How is it that Rockstar Games can claim in their promotional videos for *Red Dead Redemption* and *L.A. Noire* to recreate the experience (or processes) of the actual American West and 1940s Los Angeles, respectively? Because durable genres combined with the computational procedures and processes that comprise video games create realities for players to exist within.

Games such as *Red Dead Redemption* and *L.A. Noire* have more than "storytelling ambitions," to use Jesper Juul's characterization of game narrative.[5] The Western and its kin, hard-boiled noir, are durable genres that control gameplay and narrative progression. For example, when video game critic Harold Goldberg states that the *Grand Theft Auto* series is based on "a crazy conglomeration of all the best gangster movies," he implies that Rockstar co-founder and lead writer Dan Houser was utterly dependent on a durable genre to produce the game.[6] When Sacha Howells notes that cutscenes (short filmic sequences) give the player objectives in the game and offer causal relationships, he implies that the reason they work so well is due to the genre conventions they adhere to.[7] Clearly, literary and film genres are crucial to the game worlds that depend on them for narrative coherence. It's time to consider the social and cultural implications of making Westerns and hard-boiled noir (and, by extension, other durable genres) playable.

Why the Western and hard-boiled noir genres? Because scholars, including myself, have published rafts of research tracking the history and formation of the Western and hard-boiled noir. However, the bulk of this work is in print and film genres. A genre can't be thought of as one-dimensional, explains Steve Neale, but needs to be perceived as multifaceted and ubiquitous.[8] The Western—and to a lesser extent hard-boiled noir—is arguably one of the most multifaceted and ubiquitous of all American genres. The frontier myth has been narrativized in vast and varied ways via the mediums of fiction, film, material culture, digital games, and visual art to suit the needs of audiences, aesthetic desires, and for many other reasons across centuries. Genres do not necessarily pay attention to laws of purity but cross-breed and cross-pollinate both in content and medium: this is the "law of the law of genre."[9]

This "law of the law" is certainly true of noir, which is a notoriously broad and loose genre. A consistent refrain in any work about noir is the difficulty in defining this genre. Noir is not for genre purists, proclaim Jennifer Fay and Justice Nieland.[10] Fiction and film noir, according to Frank Krutnik, Fay and Nieland, and Dennis Broe, have worked to disrupt genre conventions more than sustain them, which is likely why noir is so difficult to pin down as a genre. This difficulty does not exist for the Western, which has a highly visible and definable iconography. Yet within the mire of fiction and film noir, there are clear forms that can be defined, and they are invariably related to the Western. While *L.A. Noire* tends to remix forms of Hollywood noir, this game world is particularly invested in the hard-boiled variety. More on the relationship between hard-boiled or "tough-guy" noir and the Western later in the introduction. For now, I'd like to focus more fully on why a rhetorical, cultural approach to genre matters.

The Power of Genre Compels You

I'm willing to bet that you were first introduced to genres in high school English classes, where genre is usually defined via categories of poetry, prose, and drama. However, those who work in communication studies and rhetoric know that genres aren't simply lists of dry and dusty categories, but instead they induce social action.[11] Genres help us to group symbols that in turn supply meaning and significance to various contexts and situations, whether we are ordering coffee, deciding how to interact with a stranger, or investigating a murder in a game world. Through genres, explains Amy Devitt, we are able to construct answers to questions posed by social and political situations and contexts.[12] Carolyn Miller argues that a genre is a fusion of rhetorical forms bound together by an internal dynamic that provides guidelines for dealing with varied rhetorical and social situations.[13] So literary genres, particularly durable ones, like the Western and hard-boiled noir, have an internal dynamic that is repeated, and through this repetition readers learn the formula of the genre and in turn gain knowledge from the formula that they can apply when needed. Therefore, literary genres have influence on social situations by giving readers a repertoire to draw from.

Durable literary genres are formed across time and circulate via the materiality of print, film, digital, and plastic cultures, narrating the ideologies that formed them in the first place across decades and even centuries. For example, both *Red Dead Redemption* and *L.A. Noire* feature player characters that are not simply the usual cisgender, white, straight males ubiquitous to gaming. Both John Marston, the outlaw-cowboy, and Jack Kelso, the hard-boiled detective, are descendants of frontiersmen, who exemplified rugged individualism, capacity for violence, stoicism, and hardness. Yet, these kinds of archetypal figures and their relationship to gameplay have not been of much interest to game studies scholars. The game studies community is still largely invested in defining genre purely as a means to categorize.

This lack of interest in the rhetorical, procedural implications of literary genre might be a hangover from the tired and well-worn narratology versus ludology debate. Alexander Galloway succinctly defines that debate as "narratologists [making the] claim that video games are simply interactive narratives, [and] ludologists [making the] claim that games must be defined separately from the concept of narrative."[14] While Galloway argues that video games need to be differentiated from other types of media, he also defines video games as "cultural object[s], bound by history and materiality."[15] I couldn't agree more, and while this critical approach has been taken up, mainly in terms of politics and gender, by such scholars as Shira Chess, Mia Consalvo, Anastasia Salter, Gerald Voorhees, and Bridget Blodgett, there is still little work, if any, on the rhetorical, historical, and material function of literary genres in game worlds.

Mark Wolf's essay "Genre and the Video Game" is perhaps the most famous and comprehensive of the early studies in genre and video games.[16] Wolf rejects the idea that games could be classified using the same standards of "iconographic" classification as film: "While some video games can be classified in a manner similar to that of films (we might say that *Outlaw* is a Western, *Space Invaders* science fiction, and *Combat* a war game), classification by iconography ignores the fundamental differences and similarities which are to be found in the player's experience of the game."[17] Wolf's point is well taken—the conventions of one media cannot be wholly used to classify another form of media—but his assertions do not take into account the rhetorical function of genre. That said, he couldn't have known in 2001 that durable genres would come to inform the procedural rhetoric of many game worlds and, in turn, profoundly influence the player's experience of the game.

Wolf's work aligns with Galloway's assertions that video games are a medium that require physical action on the part of the user for the work to exist, which separates video games from other media, such as film.[18] But are game-world Westerns and hard-boiled noir so easily isolated as video game stories, subordinate to gameplay and processes? The Western, as Steven Neale notes, is one of the few genres that can be studied via generic iconography exactly because of its clearly defined visual features.[19] Durable literary genres are more than the mediums that convey them. While the player is crucial to game worlds, this fact does not negate or change the influence of durable literary genres on either the way games operate or the ideological positioning of the player within the game.

Early work in how to classify video games was mainly fueled by a dialectical tension between video games and film. Certain critics, such as Markku Eskelinen, were not only dismissive of cutscenes but also actively resisted the reference to any twentieth-century media in the study of video games.[20]

Conversely, other critics suggested that studying the "contact and divergence" between video games and film could produce a more comprehensive and inclusive form of game criticism. Geoff King and Tanya Krzywinska use Jay David Bolter and Richard Grusin's work *Remediation* to explore the relationship between old and new media, with a particular focus on how video games borrow from film and vice versa. King and Krzywinska delineate the ways film and gameplay can create a hybrid classification system for video games, such as using the film term "milieu" to denote the fictional setting of a game.[21] While King and Krzywinska are intent on building a filmic form of game criticism, the Western has a built-in iconography generated through centuries of popular print and visual culture, translated into film, and now remediated or remixed in video games. There is a certain impossibility in denying the relevance of literary and film criticism when studying game-world Westerns and even hard-boiled noir, which has its own distinct iconography (such as the hard stare of the world-weary detective).

There's a wide range of more current genre analysis of video games, but most follow the traditional route of classification. Both David Clearwater and Thomas Apperley argue for specific modes of genre analysis, with the former advocating for a multifaceted form of genre analysis with a focus on methodology and the latter arguing for a narrow model of videogame classification that eschews reference to older forms of media.[22] These tussles over how to quantify game worlds into classification systems have value in supplying a language through which to discuss games. I'm less interested in classification or the "what" of genres and much more interested in how and why certain literary conventions populate game worlds. This seems like a good point to discuss types of Westerns and hard-boiled noir that tend to be remixed in game worlds, with a sharp eye on *Red Dead Redemption* and *L.A. Noire*.

Genre Redux

There is no doubt that *The Virginian*, published in 1902, has engendered many of the conventions associated with the Western, but how and why this novel was produced is crucial to my argument. In *The Frontier Club*, Christine Bold reorients the modern Western from its orthodox origin story as springing Athena-like from the mind of Owen Wister to its actual incarnation "by influential figures and discourses."[23] Bold's print culture and historical approach upends conventional genre studies of the Western by shifting the focus from a single author to the persistent cultural and historical discourses that produced the modern Western. For example, John Cawelti in *Six-Gun Mystique* (1971) gives Owen Wister credit for originating the modern Western via *The Virginian* and limits *The Virginian*'s influence to the "first three decades of the twentieth century."[24] Jane Tompkins similarly attributes Wister's *The Virginian* with setting "the pattern for the western in the twentieth century."[25] Richard Slotkin is closer to Bold's reconfiguration of *The Virginian* as progenitor by describing it as "the cattle range represented as a Social Darwinian laboratory," yet Slotkin still attributes creation of the novel to Wister alone.[26] More recent studies of *The Virginian*, most notably Melody Graulich's edited collection, counter Cawelti's thirty-year limit to *The Virginian*'s influence but still give Wister the credit for thinking up a novel that as of 2019 has never been out of print.[27] The modern Western is not simply birthed from Wister's *The Virginian*, but the culmination of the political and cultural will of patrician easterners, who shaped and controlled the Western formula.[28] This particular formula, which embraces the frontier myth in a postfrontier world, informs the procedural rhetoric of *Red Dead Redemption*.

The formula comprises a tenderfoot narrator; the fictionalizing of historic events to benefit the ruling classes; a laconic white cowboy; white triumphalism; oppression of women; and defense of free-market ideologies.[29] Bold harnesses this formula and its ideological underpinnings to a particular group of influential "club" men. These patrician easterners or "gentlemen hunters" included Theodore Roosevelt, U.S. president from 1901 to 1909; George Bird Grinnell, conservationist and anthropologist; Owen Wister, best-selling author; and Frederic Remington, perhaps the greatest visual artist of Western mythos. Despite their privilege, as both Bold and G. Edward White make clear, these men were threatened by progressive movements of the time: labor movements, suffragettes, and early civil rights groups (for both Indigenous and black communities) were demanding shared resources and power.[30]

Frontier club members perceived the West as their private playground and a capitalist resource.[31] They weren't alone, as "most popular Westerns in the early twentieth century narrativize the transformation and exploitation of the landscape, animals, and peoples of the West into consumable material for capitalist appetites."[32] Through control of the mass print publishing industry, frontier club members ensured that their version of the West and its mythos reached the masses (and it's never stopped doing so). Those who dared oppose eastern ranching (or corporate) interests in newspaper or magazine articles saw those articles disappear. Wister stamped the Western with the values and interests of the frontier club members, which centers on protecting white, male, patrician privilege in the name of democracy.[33] With cisgender, straight, white males as the default identity in the majority of game worlds, it's no wonder this form of Western, which I'll dub the "frontier Western" from here on out, is the one most often remediated in game worlds.[34]

Closely related to the frontier Western is the hard-boiled detective genre, which "began as an abstraction of the essential elements of the frontier myth."[35] Slotkin explains that the detective hero is not unlike the Virginian in that he is a man who understands crime and can consort with criminals or "savages," but he also has a sense of justice. Slotkin provides one of the most in-depth excavations of the hard-boiled genre, linking it to Charles Siringo's autobiographical writings of his experience as a cowboy turned Pinkerton detective.[36] In *A Cowboy Detective* (1912), Siringo creates a "hard-boiled" detective character who has no problem interacting with those on the other side of the law and using whatever means necessary to get the job done, which is reminiscent of the Virginian, who hangs a friend turned rustler because he has to do what he has to do.[37] This violent pragmatism (common to the Romantic roots of the Western, where the hero has seemingly natural moral acuity) also describes Jack Kelso, the hard-boiled player character in *L.A. Noire*. He kills a former friend whose traumatic war experience drove him to madness and violence.[38]

While Siringo characterizes himself as a "man of the people," he despises the "savagery" of strikers and anarchists, allowing Siringo to at once identify with his readers as "everyman" and in turn indoctrinate them into a frontier worldview where self-reliance, individualism, and (white) rugged masculinity are prized. However, unlike *The Virginian*, in which the elite, represented by Judge Henry, are all-knowing and benign aristocrats dutifully looking after the underclasses, everyone is corrupt and corruptible in Siringo's urban environment, except the detective figure. This perspective describes *L.A. Noire* to a tee. The hard-boiled detective's traits are directly related to the traditional frontier hero, and like his ancestor, he also facilitates progress whenever and wherever he can. These genre conventions are part of the procedural rhetoric of both *Red Dead Redemption* and *L.A. Noire*. Both game worlds incorporate a socially Darwinist landscape where "survival of the fittest" is euphemistically described as a "meritocracy."[39]

This social Darwinist landscape where "the best man wins" can also be described as an American form of neoliberalism, which desires to "bring all human action in the domain of the market," no matter what the consequence to equality and civil rights.[40] The game story in both *Red Dead Redemption* and *L.A. Noire* requires players to perform as reluctant protagonists whose main goals (expressed via gameplay) are to protect the small rancher or the little guy on the urban frontier, but both fail in the face of corporate and political interests. *Wait*, you might be thinking, *this doesn't sound like a socially Darwinist, neoliberal landscape. This seems more akin to a progressive storyline.* That might seem so, but remember the "law of the law" of genre; these frontier game worlds adapt the Western and hard-boiled genres to suit the tastes of patriarchal gaming conventions, where the hero must be a "persecuted minority." This fantasy of persecution, where the white male savior rescues, usually, the damsel in distress, dovetails with the conventions of the cowboy and hard-boiled detective figures.[41] Both the cowboy and the hard-boiled detective must fight "savage" enemies to save not just the girl but ways of life, and this is what's at stake in both *Red Dead Redemption* and *L.A. Noire*.

In *Red Dead Redemption*, John Marston reluctantly leaves his ranch, the symbol of his recuperation from outlaw to ranch owner, to rescue his family. His main mission is to hunt down former gang members and appease the government agents who are holding his family hostage. However, Marston is often called upon to protect private property from rustlers and "savages."

Most missions, divided into chapters, involve Marston admitting that the government and corporations are to blame for making life difficult for small ranching and farming operations; however, instead of attacking the corporate culprits, he punishes the rustlers, Indians, and banditos (aka those who resist) for daring to disrupt "civilized" settlers.

Similarly, one of two main player characters in *L.A. Noire*, police detective Cole Phelps, consistently states that he "wants to make the world a better place by enforcing the law," but he can't understand that the law does not apply to those of a certain class and wealth level. The other player character, hard-boiled detective Jack Kelso, does. Much like Marston, Phelps is disillusioned by his discovery of corruption and pays with his life for resisting the corrupt status quo. Kelso understands that it's pointless to fight against economic disparity and other social ills. While these game worlds are bleak, they fulfill the ideological promise of their print and film ancestors to quell anxieties over economic, racial, and gender inequalities through the white triumphalism of their white male player characters.

This ideological promise of the Western and noir is expressed via forms of literary and filmic realism, romanticism, and naturalism. This fact may have literary and film scholars asking why I don't move beyond realism. Part of the reason is the sheer number of narratives and forms that comprise the episodic nature of game worlds. There are many side missions (akin to vignettes) in both *Red Dead Redemption* and *L.A. Noire* that incorporate the gritty social determinism of naturalism or even the supernatural elements of magical realism or gothic fiction. In short, I simply can't discuss all the literary and filmic forms that appear in these massive game worlds. To keep this book a manageable length, I decided to stick with discussing realism, particularly capitalist realism per se, rather than analyzing the larger implications of realism as a historical movement and form. I hope others will fill in the gaps I was unable to, such as investigating how naturalism and romanticism influence gameplay and the concept of choice and freedom in game worlds. How does sentimentality define agency in game worlds? Why do American genres dominate game-world storylines? In other words, now that the narratology and ludology debate has finally been put to rest, let's use every available analytical tool we have to study game worlds, which are, quite frankly, the primary means by which stories are told in the twenty-first century.

Chapter Overview

Chapter 1 examines how the frontier Western has shaped *Red Dead Redemption*'s game world and in turn the cultural work *Red Dead Redemption* performs as a twenty-first century frontier Western. As the reformed outlaw-cowboy John Marston, the player rides horses, does ranch chores, and defends ranchers. On this ludo-frontier, Marston successfully completes missions in which he must protect predominantly white settler ranchers and homesteaders from encroaching change by corporate interests, government interventions, racialized enemies, and technology. However, he also works on behalf of the government and its corporate sponsors to usher in the end the frontier. This chapter argues that the procedural rhetoric of this ludo-frontier operates as a safety valve for the pressures brought to bear by the continued repercussions of the 2008 economic collapse.

In chapter 2 players cross the border into Nuevo Paraiso (New Paradise), which is *Red Dead Redemption*'s ludic parody of a historical Mexico. Marston along with Landon Ricketts, outlaw turned self-proclaimed lawman, encourage the player through gameplay, such as duels and rescue missions, that they are vastly superior to their Mexican counterparts. Set during the Mexican Revolution, the geography of this game world positions the borderlands as literally below New Austin. While New Austin suffers from crime and corruption, Nuevo Paraiso is a hopelessly corrupt, poverty-stricken, and crime-ridden region. Through gameplay and cutscenes, the player is immersed within white neocolonial triumphalism.

After defining the American way of life through opposition and negation in Nuevo Paraiso, the player returns to New Austin. The procedural rhetoric of the game demands that players engage in a type of "Indian removal" in Tall Trees, which is adjacent to the urban sprawl of West Elizabeth. This area reflects the political state of Indigenous peoples within the boundaries of the real-life United States, who sit in a kind of limbo, according to Mark Rifkin, at once encompassed by U.S. law and excluded from it.[42] In chapter 3 I argue that this liminal state is performed in Tall Trees through the nonplayer character "Indians," who are excluded from the main geographical areas of the game and are hunted in the game by government agents, including Marston. The ludo-colonial missions set in Tall Trees prove Rifkin's and Michael Yellow Bird's arguments that neocolonialism thrives in American popular culture and supports the continued colonization of Indigenous lands.[43]

The book then moves from the interplay between the frontier Western and *Red Dead Redemption* to the urban frontiers of Hollywood noir, with a particular focus on the hard-boiled detective genre. Both the frontier Western and its hard-boiled kin build a specific state of fantasy in which whiteness is yoked to neoliberal forms of masculinity. Chapter 4 argues that this game world persuades players to privilege a certain kind rugged, frontier-style masculinity through one of the main player characters, Jack Kelso. For much of the game, players believe the central player character is Cole Phelps, a war veteran who joins the Los Angeles police force and rises through the ranks; however, players eventually learn that Phelps is not hard-boiled but its opposite: intellectual and liberal. As a true frontier hero, Kelso doesn't trust authority but intrinsically knows that civilization must be protected. Through missions and collectible narrative elements, such as newspapers, players learn not only that the height of masculine potency is the hard-boiled detective but also that his rugged individualism accepts neoliberalism and corruption as inevitable.

The hard-boiled detective can't perform his rugged masculinity without women who can define his potency and power. In *L.A. Noire* American white women, as a category, have a certain function beyond simply defining men as men. White women in particular, though not exclusively, have consistently operated in American literature and culture as metonymic substitutions for the nation, often appearing as part of a signifying chain of meaning that defines (particularly middle-class) womanhood as inextricably connected with the American home and domesticity. This symbolic function is continued in a disturbing fashion via gameplay when Phelps must chase a serial killer who kills married women, thereby destroying the family home. White women have traditionally been the moral compass of the American home, but each of these women (scripted into gameplay as nonplayer characters) are represented as dissatisfied with their middle-class lifestyles, drinking heavily and behaving "immorally," thereby rendering themselves and their families vulnerable to attack by evil.

Finally, chapter 6 shows how the central plot line of this game world, revealed in the final missions, ties together all of the previous plotlines, which are shared through collectible newspapers scattered throughout the game. This central plotline narrates the struggle to sustain a stable family life, resist the temptations of socialism, and accumulate the markers of success (e.g., a home and property). Phelps and Kelso discover that one of the men who served under them in World War II, Ira Hogeboom, who suffers from post-traumatic stress disorder, has been manipulated by his doctor to burn down houses built specifically for GIs. The scheme involves the highest levels of government and also corporate leaders, who agree to build the homes on the future site of the infamous Los Angeles freeways. The houses are insured for much more than they are worth to line the pockets of corporate and government stakeholders and shortchange war veterans. Through gameplay, players gather narrative clues that reveal there is no justice in a hard-boiled noir world or, perhaps by extension, in their own worlds.

Initially, I set out to show the overlapping and interconnected nature of durable genres and game worlds. My central question was quite simple: how do literary genres influence the procedural rhetoric of a video game? What I discovered is that durable literary genres direct players' experience of the game world. My hope is that this book encourages others, including researchers, instructors, students, and gamers, to consider the rhetorical, cultural, and social implications of the literary genres that inform game worlds. Perhaps it's time to consider that if the "law of the law of genre" is to resist genre purity and embrace genre diversity, then, to echo Bold, other forms of the Western and hard-boiled noir need to elbow aside certain conventions and offer players more options. What might it be like to play as a black cowboy modeled after Nat Love or as an Indigenous woman— such as Mourning Dove's eponymous hero in *Cogewea*? How about a game world where the avatar is Marvel's acerbic hard-boiled detective Jessica Jones? These forms of Western and noir already exist; they just need to be remediated.

1 The Game and the Nation

Legacies of the Frontier Western

At the beginning of a chapter sequence in *The Virginian* (1902) aptly titled "The Game and the Nation," Owen Wister defines American democracy, equality, and social mobility as types of win/lose conditions in a national game:

It was through the Declaration of Independence that we Americans acknowledged the eternal inequality of man. For by it we abolished a cut-and-dried aristocracy. We had seen little men artificially held up in high places, and great men artificially held down in low places, and our own justice-loving hearts abhorred this violence to human nature. Henceforth, we decreed that every man should thenceforth have equal liberty to find his own level. By this very decree we acknowledged and gave freedom to true aristocracy, saying, "Let the best man win, whoever he is." Let the best man win! That is America's word. That is true democracy. And true democracy and true aristocracy are one and the same thing.[1]

Gary Scharnhorst has called this infamous quotation an "elitist political credo" that is enacted through a strategic game played by the eponymous main character, the Virginian, to defeat his nemesis (and employee), Trampas.[2]

The greenhorn narrator, who ventriloquizes Wister here, does not mean any "man" can win but that only cisgender, straight, white men can. Christine Bold describes this novel as "whitewashed," and certainly, the "eternal inequality" referred to by the greenhorn narrator affects not only Trampas but also those who aren't invited to play, such as Scipio le Moyne, camp cook and ally to the Virginian, who "carries the marks of African American identity."[3] His sycophancy is only matched by Trampas's violent resistance to the Virginian's apparent natural aristocracy.

Trampas wants the other cowboys to leave the outfit run by the Virginian (as foreman) and head out to California to join the Gold Rush. The Gold Rush offers them the opportunity to escape managerial capitalism and become, in a sense, managers of their own fate. The Virginian crushes his opponent, subdues the cowboy laborers, and fulfills the prophecy to "let the best man win!" Owen Wister and his patrician friends—dubbed the "frontier club" by Bold—created a mythic world that has formed the frontier Western and where a certain kind of "eternal inequality" can reign. This world not only mirrors their power but reinforces it.[4] In other words, the game is rigged.

Red Dead Redemption and the Frontier Western

The Virginian mends the cracks in the master narrative of westering and exceptionalism that began to show clearly in the late nineteenth century. In his 1881 treatise, General James Sanks Brisbin famously lamented, "When the West is settled, what then?"[5] Frederick Jackson Turner confirmed Brisbin's anxieties about the closing of the frontier in 1893 by stating that because the U.S. census could not confirm a geographical line that indicated where civilization ended and the frontier begins, western expansion and therefore the frontier no longer existed. However, Turner also argued that because the frontier "has been fundamental in the economic, political, and social characteristics of the American people and in their conceptions of their destiny," the frontier myth lives on as a master genre.[6] Turner publicly aired out the musty narrative of the frontier myth and gave citizens strong reasons to invest in the ideologies of the frontier. In turn, Wister and his frontier club brethren narrativized Turner's thesis from their own ideological standpoint, produced *The Virginian*, and ensured that their version of the frontier myth lives on in print, film, and now game worlds.

Fast-forward to 2010: *Red Dead Redemption* incorporates the frontier club formula, redeploying the philosophies of inequality that Wister and his frontier club peers saw as the natural state of human existence. *The Virginian* is a "frontier club western," explains Bold, that articulates the ideological platform of early twentieth-century "patrician easterners," such as President Teddy Roosevelt, anthropologist George Bird Grinnell, and Senator Henry Cabot Lodge. This group of wealthy white males "clinched the [narrative] formula that has long served as the most popular face of America . . . yoking the genre to their interests in hunting and conservation, open-range ranching, mass publishing, Jim Crow segregation, immigration restriction, and American Indian assimilation."[7] Several of these interests have been entrenched in the game-world frontiers of *Red Dead Redemption* and are narrated via its cowboy-outlaw hero, John Marston.

The frontier Western brands America through a certain type of American masculinity: the "rugged individual."[8] Embodied by the cowboy figure, rugged masculinity combines atavistic coarseness and violence with preternatural abilities, offering nearly limitless access to the benefits of American capitalism.[9] Linda Tuhiwai Smith (Ngāti Awa and Ngāti Porou, Māori) calls this form of Western selfhood "predatory individualism."[10] Mark Anderson explains that the frontier Western (meaning a Western that fully embraces the frontier myth) typically triumphs archetypal masculine Americana (bravery, whiteness, self-control).[11] This exceptionalist version of masculinity has waxed and waned in popularity over the last hundred years but has continued to "make the man," to paraphrase Lee Clark Mitchell, in print, film, and game worlds.

Allegorical Spandex, Capitalist Realism, and Cowboys

This near-seamless remediation or reproduction of the frontier Western across many forms of media can be attributed to the most popular form of narrative expression: realism. Realism models an intelligible and plausible fictional world for a mass audience and in turn positions the audience within that world. Realism reproduces everyday life in minute detail, increasing the modality or truth value of a narrative. Westerns tend use a form of realism that oscillates "between myth and history," explains Alexandra Keller, which is not simply a mimetic representation of history but becomes history itself through its "realist aesthetic that naturalizes information so that it *appears* historically accurate, even if it is not."[12]

Catherine Belsey argues that realism does not simply represent but interpellates the audience or player into a range of discourses that enables the subject (audience or player) to understand their position within a social and cultural order. In less academic terms, we are shaped by the forms of language that surround us.[13] We are "hailed" or called into our social positions by those with the power to do so. Durable literary genres tell us the value of certain social positions and who has the power to control others linguistically, physically, and therefore socially. In the frontier Western, the cowboy figure is at the apex. Realism is a powerful form of storytelling with dangerous implications. Put another way, "stories are wondrous things," explains Cherokee Greek author and scholar Thomas King, "but they are also dangerous."[14]

In game worlds, the dangers of realism become much more apparent because players believe they are making choices, defeating enemies, and achieving goals in a replication of a reality. They are "on the holodeck," to borrow Janet Murray's *Star Trek* metaphor.[15] To explain by way of example, Harold Goldberg was duped when he described *Red Dead Redemption* as a game that offers reputable information about the American West: *Red Dead Redemption* is "an understated history lesson of a time when the United States was in utter transition in everything from politics to religion to technology."[16] If an erudite and seasoned game critic like Goldberg can be convinced that this remediated frontier Western offers any semblance of a history lesson, then there is a strong likelihood that most players are equally inculcated.

One of the questions I've been asked at conferences and research seminars is whether the developers knew that the form of Western they were using encoded multiple layers of oppression. In other words, if Dan and

Sam Houser knew the origins of the frontier club Western and its ideological underpinnings, would they have used it as the internal engine of their game narrative? Goldberg explains that Rockstar claims to be the bad boy of the game industry and articulates "Palahniukesque anarchic energy."[17] Therefore, when players enter a Rockstar Game, they (we) expect resistance to a status quo that seems to value economic disparity, white triumphalism, and unfettered progress, but this is not what players encounter. Instead, players are visually dazzled with incredible graphics and cool characters, which is the "allegorical spandex" of realism that Houser cheekily defines as Rockstar's philosophy of game design.[18] While Rockstar's name may be apropos to its bedazzled image, *Red Dead Redemption* follows the mantra of late capitalism: protests are futile and government intervention is unwanted. The invisible hand of the market and fate will regulate everyday life. As winners in the game of neoliberal capitalism, the Houser brothers are members of the twenty-first century frontier club, benefiting from the philosophy of unequal equality.

Mark Fisher calls neoliberals "capitalist realists par excellence," paring down the state to "its core military and police functions." *Red Dead Redemption* is a space where players are immersed in capitalist realism. Belief, faith, and even democracy are corrupt and corruptible. Gameplay is centered on the almighty dollar. Animals are valued for their skins, bounties can be collected from criminals, and saving settlers from peril results in monetary reward. This is a world where all is subsumed to capitalist impulses, furthering a general malaise that nothing is new, nothing has changed, and the end of history is upon us.[19] Fisher explains that this paradigm is mainly expressed through the neo-noir genre common to the late twentieth and twenty-first centuries. He cites a number of Quentin Tarantino films, which, of course, owe a debt to the frontier Western, in which capitalist enterprise is heralded.

The frontier Western is well suited to capitalist realism, with its dehistoricizing of Indigenous and racial histories, sanitizing of the American West, and transforming of the cowboy to either a laborer or member of the managerial class. As primarily a frontier Western, *Red Dead Redemption* offers a specifically American vision of capitalist realism, initiating the player into a landscape where they can perform brute (white) masculinity

1. JOHN MARSTON HERDING CATTLE. *RED DEAD REDEMPTION*.

and experience rugged individualism. The main agent of this frontier philosophy is the reformed gunslinger-cowboy-outlaw John Marston, who furthers and more importantly rejuvenates what the narrator trumpets in *The Virginian* as "the *eternal inequality* of man."[20] As Marston, players are only able to move through the plot lines if they resolve the crises they encounter. These "crises" are contained in missions, which are directed via the conventions of the frontier Western.

For example, Marston is saved by a small ranch owner, Bonnie MacFarlane, after he confronts his former gang at Fort Mercer, where he is shot and left for dead. When he wakes up at the MacFarlane ranch, Bonnie explains that his treatment cost fifteen dollars, clearly a significant sum, and he promises to repay his debt (most gameplay is generally rewarded by a dollar amount or exchange of goods). He pays her by becoming her ranch hand, going on patrol with her, breaking horses, and herding cattle. That is, players embodied as Marston complete these chores as part of gameplay, earning money for this cowboy labor.

These missions are not part of the main plot, which comprises Marston's quest to save his family and land by capturing or assassinating his former gang members at the behest of government law enforcement. The plot unfolds through chapters, which contain game play and cutscenes (short film sequences).

Red Dead Redemption embodies frontier ideals performatively. Game worlds have the narrative capacity to engage "myth models," which are the "powerful, paradigmatic myths that serve as the models for the construction of similar myths, such as the myth of the noble savage that informs other, parallel, or derivative myths of primitivism."[21] The frontier is certainly a paradigmatic myth that has been used to model derivative myths of American exceptionalism and capitalist, neoliberal ideals in American popular culture, from space Westerns to vampire stories. In this game world, the frontier myth takes on a particularly powerful form as a "locus of symbol and action and of image and (embodied) motion." That is, video games are not simply "a set of eyes fixed on a screen" but also a bodily performance of the game action, which creates a much more powerful connection between the narrative and player and perhaps reopens arguments concerning the function of narratives to shape reality across time.[22]

Paul Ricoeur argues that narratives have the ability to produce physical or behavioral actions from the audience because textual action and lived experience are difficult to define and separate. So difficult, in fact, that we require modifiers and modal auxiliaries to help separate fact from fiction; for example, if we are being told a story that does not have the proper modifiers that categorize it as fact or fiction, we will ask "is that true?"[23] Based on Ricoeur's assertion that factual or fictional narratives are the main conduits through which humans interpret the world, the ability of game worlds, like *Red Dead Redemption*, to engage multiple levels of literacy, including symbol, film, image, text, and performance, has major social and cultural implications. What is so appealing about a form of Western developed primarily for an early twentieth-century American audience?

The United States in the early twentieth century and early twenty-first century have much in common: both periods engage the frontier as a space where history and myth coalesce to create a cohesive, exceptional, and normative nation that could be imagined as a reality.[24] Marston must repair the fractures in property ownership that occur across the landscape of New Austin, the fictional state in which a third of the game is set. In this space, counter-publics, such as labor movements, can be dealt with in a way that acknowledges that while the nation may be economically and morally bankrupt, it's better than the alternative, which is represented by the squalor and degradation south of the New Austin border in Nuevo Paraiso (an obvious parody of Mexico). Marston, as the cowboy-outlaw, acts both as hero to the little guy and an agent of the state: he is both an outlaw and conformist. This ontological paradox enables him to narrate and make sense of social, cultural, racial, and political contradictions.[25] Marston often complains bitterly about the injustice of the government or railway companies, yet he conforms to their demands, albeit under pressure. He enacts Teddy Roosevelt's masculine ideal of frontier hardiness, which requires the frontier cowboy hero "to preserve life and the lives of others," even if he does not always agree with the ideological underpinnings of his mission.[26] The cowboy figure has primarily operated to create epistemic stability and preservation in times of upheaval, according to Mitchell:

> To wonder why cowboys were translated into such mythic status ("the Cowboy") or to ask why the West emerged when it did is to enter into vexed historical terrain. The simplest explanation involves the collective response to industrial capitalism: the West once again as escape valve for eastern tensions and psychological pressures . . . with the transition to an urban economy and the pressures of a newly modernized society, the allure of a more stable, agrarian working culture is not hard to imagine, perhaps especially since the frontier had come to seem irrevocably closed. In an era of massive immigration, urbanization, and production-line labor, the West could be imagined as the "premodern world that Americans had lost."[27]

The cultural work of the American frontier in the early twentieth century that Mitchell outlines here continues in game-world Westerns. They quell anxieties that white male privilege (born out of early twentieth-century frontier ideals) is foundering under the strain of the post-2008 financial collapse, continued economic disparity, and a perceived loss of cisgender, straight, white male privilege.[28]

From the rise of the Tea Party to the 2016 Republican Party presidential primaries and the subsequent election of Donald J. Trump, the framing of an authentic American identity in terms of whiteness, rugged masculinity, and heteronormativity pervades American public life. As Vincent Cheng explains, contemporary Western nations "still cling to notions of authenticity and authentic identities."[29] This belief in the authenticity of whiteness perpetuated by the frontier Western has allowed for crimes to be committed against those deemed different from the norm. Anastasia Salter and Bridget Blodgett argue that toxic forms of white masculinity are furthered by mass media and game-world conventions.[30] Therefore, the frontier Western and game-world conventions are well suited to each other.

Foreclosing the Frontier

Bundled with the cowboy figure are ideologies of property and ownership, explains Victoria Lamont; in the late nineteenth century, there was an "entrepreneurial fantasy of limitless economic expansion" and a "discourse of private property" in the West that firmly entrenched corporate hierarchies of labor and ownership.[31] Marston, a former outlaw who proves himself an honest cowboy, must defeat rustlers, herd cattle, break horses, and save the MacFarlanes' small ranch from bankruptcy. Most of the problems various characters suffer are caused by corporate railway and ranching interests in the East that are supported by the government and enforced by the Bureau of Investigation. Both Marston and Marshal Leigh Johnson, the long-serving lawman of Armadillo, New Austin, solve the various problems (via missions) caused by big business and government, but they also work for the government and the railway, respectively.

Further, the government and railway are bringing rapid technological change to the West: Marston and the marshal awkwardly use telephones and see motorcars being transported by paddleboat, which mirrors the economic instability and rapid technological change that the United States (and many Western nations) are currently experiencing. This game world naturalizes the disparities between rich and poor, depletion in standards of living, and, most importantly, sustains perpetual mourning for a lost way of life while offering no alternative except a melancholic state. Marston mourns the closing of the frontier, which parallels the loss of property and status that many American households have suffered and may continue to suffer. According to RealtyTrac and cnbc.com, 1 in every 611 housing units in the United States in July 2011 was repossessed by the bank or other financial institution. Even though these statistics are down slightly from the previous year, this reprieve, of sorts, is only due to interventions from the federal and state level to stave off foreclosures.[32] These statistics indicate that the nation and its privileged, property-owning citizens have suffered a traumatic wounding. If, as Amy Kaplan and Lora Romero theorize, the American home is a fetishized space that encompasses both the familial home and the nation, then the steady rate of foreclosures have materially damaged the structural integrity of the American mythos. The "ragged edges of the Real," to draw from Cornel West, have been exposed.[33] Indeed, this multifaceted loss of material and spiritual property, or to loosely paraphrase Slavoj Žižek, a sublime loss in the stability of exceptionalist ideology, places the American subject in a state of flux between mourning and melancholia.[34] Arguably, the entire nation has been in a continual state of mourning since 9/11, and the collapse has encouraged this perennial mourning, which is a pathological state (much like melancholia) that can afflict a national group. Vamik Volkan argues that entire social groups can be invested with entitlement ideologies through which certain cultural groups will violently try to mitigate the loss they have suffered by taking back what they feel is rightfully theirs.[35]

The question is, then, why do the majority of Americans passively accept foreclosures, job loss, and economic disparity, among other social facts, despite nationally entrenched promises of entitlement to life, liberty, and the pursuit of happiness? Perhaps the high tolerance for inequality and loss, even the loss of homes—one of the prime symbols of national stability and privileged identity—can be linked in part to the idea that the strenuous life, replete with suffering, is a necessary part of fulfilling normative American identity. *Red Dead Redemption* rescues white, middle-class, heteronormative identity in the form of small ranch owners and homesteaders and through these representations teaches its players that suffering, loss, and rapid technological change are simply part of life. This game world naturalizes and therefore depoliticizes the economic downturn. This playable frontier operates as a safety valve for the pressures brought to bear on American citizenry by the continued repercussions of the 2008 collapse and other national upheavals.

This game world relieves the pressures of economic instability and disparity through the participatory nature of gameplay, which offers epistemic and ontological stability. A video game engages the player on multiple levels: as a performer, a reader, and a viewer who must decode the game world in order to progress. If the player can decode each mission or plot conflict successfully, then they can move to another mission, one step closer to the story's promised rewards. In each of these plots, the player as Marston must defend, violently if necessary, the edicts of capitalism, rugged masculinity, and white triumphalism. *Red Dead Redemption*, therefore, does not simply fulfill a nostalgic dream of American identity through the "was" of the West but operates as a cultural placeholder of "authenticity and attribution."[36]

Marston (and other rugged white men in the game) group, define, and differentiate various identities from one another with the authority vested in them through their status as cisgender, white, straight cowboys. Marston defines the contours of normative identity and its attendant ideals of property and ownership through his interactions with various stock characters, namely Bonnie MacFarlane and Marshal Johnson.[37] The marshal and Bonnie are the two main nonplayer characters (NPCs) with whom Marston interacts in New Austin before he meets with NPCs who facilitate his journey into Mexico, where the plot shifts more drastically toward issues of colonization, immigration, and border politics.

The initial missions at Bonnie's ranch describe a political landscape that is in many ways reminiscent of the class struggles that occurred in Johnson County, Wyoming, in the late nineteenth century while also articulating longings for the myth of a Jeffersonian natural space. Marston desires the "real West," where people can be practically free from governmental control. While Marston is the idealist, Bonnie is a materialist, answering, "Where did you get that romanticized drivel out of? Novels? Those days are long gone, if they ever existed. . . . Businessmen are the new cowboys." In this metafictional exchange, the frontier is both mythic in Marston's view and historically grounded through Bonnie's reference to the eastern corporate ranching interests that want to drive her family from their land.

Bonnie is a curious NPC. She is identified as a cisgender female, but she is also a type of masculine female. Bonnie is not "the rejected scraps of dominant masculinity [who exists] in order that male masculinity might appear to be the real thing."[38] Rather, Bonnie, as the pants-wearing ranch owner, is insightful and resourceful and understands that the motivating force behind civilizing the frontier is profit. Marston poetically states as he explains his final goal that he must "end one life so another can survive." Bonnie, in turn, translates Marston's frontier romanticism into historical materialism, noting sardonically that "civilization is a beautiful thing, Mr. Marston."

Marston does not answer to the foreman of the ranch, except to receive pay for keeping the peace; instead, he receives his orders from Bonnie, who is grateful to Marston not because she can be his signifying term but because her own ranch hands are not as productive as Marston: they are not as ruggedly masculine and therefore not as capable as he. Bonnie's and Marston's relationship is economically rather than romantically based. Marston owes Bonnie money and his life, both of which are intertwined. However, I do not want to suggest that this game world is feminist, because it isn't. Rather, Bonnie is simply the masculine-female version of the rugged individual.

Bonnie's performance of rugged individualism is born out of necessity: her brother fled east and her father is frail. She is a cowgirl entrepreneur, representing, in part, a "modern congruence between masculinity and liberal individual feminism," but she is also a signifier of rugged neoliberalism.[39] Unlike the other female NPCs in the game, such as the pastor's daughter Jenny, who believes God will save her from dying of tuberculosis on the frontier, Bonnie evolved into her rugged individualism through her work on the ranch. Once a young lady educated by a governess, she is now a masculine female who does not cry or exhibit sentimental emotions: she yells at her employees and barks orders. Therefore, she is not masquerading or "playing" at being male; rather, she enacts rugged individualism to dominate others in her employ.

However, when she enters the domestic sphere, Bonnie may still wear pants, but she defers her masculine power to her father. She serves Marston and her father tea as Marston learns the MacFarlane family history, which involves more suffering than triumph. MacFarlane lists the misfortunes he and his family have met with on the frontier, including drought and smallpox, both of which led to the deaths of several MacFarlane children. Despite the hardship, MacFarlane claims he wouldn't live anywhere else, and considering that New Austin is an avatar for the U.S. national sphere, this assertion is hyperbolically patriotic.

Marston wins MacFarlane over with his honesty and forthrightness, causing MacFarlane to ask Marston to break horses and as payment receive one in exchange. Of course, breaking horses is a form of gameplay integrated into this frontier Western. While they ride out to the pasture, the conversation continues: MacFarlane asserts that technological changes, government interference, and "anything else that civilizes a man" are worse menaces than any outlaw. Marston agrees with MacFarlane, and this would seem to be a genuine act of resistance against neoliberal ideals by two specimens of frontier masculinity, but Bonnie's pleas for the men to stop talking politics and "enjoy the ride" put an end to the conversation. Bonnie's position as a domestic, civilizing force gives her the authority to assert her manifest domesticity, to use Amy Kaplan's phrase, and depoliticize the conversation, thereby subordinating dissent to propriety.[40]

However, once Bonnie is away from her father's presence, she resumes her role as employer and gives Marston quite a few missions to fulfill. Bonnie does not follow Annette Kolodny's model of feminine responses to the frontier: she is not a cultivator.[41] Bonnie is interested in getting work done around the ranch, at which Marston excels, even surpassing Bonnie's foreman. In fact, *Red Dead Redemption* can be called a game world in which players do not play but work, perfecting their role in the frontier marketplace as the cowboy laborer. The lack of "play" in most video games indicates that these games are a form of social control, thereby performing the opposite function of role playing, "which [performs] critical, social, and psychological functions while being formally divorced from social reality." As cultural critics such as Peter Stallybrass and Allen White (building on Mikhail Bakhtin's work) have shown, "simulative play, like carnival, allows the glimpse of rearranged social systems while not directly impacting the systems themselves."[42]

In contrast, argues David Golumbia, current role-playing games demand that players fulfill tasks before being able to attain the ability to reach another level in the game.[43] In *Red Dead Redemption*, a player can counter the goals of the game—for example, Marston can shoot Bonnie's cowboys—but he will be breaking the cowboy code instituted via the frontier Western. His criminal behavior is literally costly in that he will have a bounty on his head and in turn be unable to progress through the game world effectively. Therefore, punishment for countering genre conventions is part of gameplay. When Marston works at Bonnie's ranch and follows genre conventions like a good cowboy, he gains access to a rifle that is required to successfully complete other missions.

This game world restricts actions that go against the cowboy code of honor. Further, hierarchies of labor are kept in place as Marston completes the tasks he must to regain his property. As Mitchell reiterates, Westerns enact forms of social control and *Red Dead Redemption* is not the exception. *Red Dead Redemption* teaches a type of performative literacy in which players enact the ideals of the frontier Western:

> The player pursues something like what a consumer of genre fiction pursues, namely knowledge of the complete future extent of the narrative and its details, and as in a generic mystery novel, the reusability of such a generic narrative is circumscribed (which is not to deny that many players, like mystery novel readers, enjoy replaying sequences whose details are well-known to them). This resemblance of FPSs [first-person shooters] and other games to genre fiction accounts in part for the attraction of narratological methods for game analysis. But what is missing in most FPS games is the rest of the material one finds in the typical narratives read by those who value literature, which is to say, *the complex individual and relationship identifications* that make literature not simply a sequence of events but a version of human engagement. Few people play computer games for their *narrative richness* or for their resemblance to the *complex human events at the representation of which novels, films, and even television have always been adept.*[44]

Golumbia's commentary was clearly produced before game worlds had reached a level of graphic and narrative sophistication where, indeed,

2. GAMEPLAY ICONS. *RED DEAD REDEMPTION.*

"complex individual relationships and identifications," "narrative richness," and "complex human events" are the norm. While *Red Dead Redemption* is clearly a frontier Western, it is also a bodily experience in which events are not simply read and seen but also *done*. The player holds a controller and manipulates a complex set of buttons in a certain order to control Marston's actions while looking at the screen and reading the instructions at the top left, which act as an omniscient narrator, and a map at lower left that allows the player to know where Marston is in the frontier landscape. These over-lapping activities that are necessary for the player to successfully engage with the game are "powerfully performative ... with both intersubjective and interobjective dimension[s]."[45]

This performative frame that governs the relationship between proce-dural rhetoric and player leaves the player much more susceptible to the ideological stance of the game world. While game worlds like that of *Red*

Dead Redemption are usually criticized for extreme violence (which is a convention of the Western genre anyway), the more pressing point is the ability of game worlds to move beyond the register of print or film narrative interaction and into the register of performance and performativity. Performativity moves beyond Cartesian duality and explores how the body and mind function to connect a person with their epistemological and ontological reality. There is no simple distinction between "*really doing* and being and *not really* doing or being." That is, a performer in a play may be asked to read a newspaper as part of a performance, but if the actor really reads the newspaper, have they stopped performing?[46] Therefore, when a player of any gender, race, or sexuality takes on the rugged masculinity of John Marston, they are highly susceptible to the ideologies at play, so to speak.

These ideologies are centered on conforming to neoliberal values, which require the correct performance of rugged individuality. Indeed, neoliberalism and the frontier mythos cannot be separated, as noted by David Harvey's description of how U.S. neoliberalism invaded Iraqi economic policy: "[Paul] Bremer [head of the Coalition Provisional Authority] invited the Iraqis, in short, to ride their horse of freedom straight into the neoliberal corral."[47] These kinds of analogies speak to the power of the frontier myth to translate neoliberal processes.

Marston's adventures as a cowboy hero at Bonnie's ranch enforce ideals concerning labor hierarchies and natural ability that is reminiscent of the Virginian's role as the natural aristocrat, whose ability to gain economic independence depends on his performance as a rugged cisgender, straight, white male. However, unlike the Virginian, Marston is a former outlaw who has recuperated and become part of the mainstream. His face is testament to his initial recuperation: heavily scarred, Marston has clearly been a part of the Western genre convention of convalescence. Whereas Mitchell argues that the convalescence scene displays men being restored to their male bodies, I believe there is more than gender recuperation at stake in *Red Dead Redemption*, and likely other versions of the popular Western.[48]

To convalesce is to move from one ontological and epistemological state to another: from sickness to health, figuratively and literally. This process reverberates with Wendy Brown's question regarding why those who do not benefit from the neoliberal project do not simply opt out of neoliberalism and pursue an "emancipatory democratic project."[49] When Marston confronts Bill Williamson, a former member of his gang, at Fort Mercer, he is the honest homesteader who is shot by those who destroy private property and corporate interests: the outlaws. His recuperation requires that he "attach" his wounding not to the government policies and corporate greed that created the outlaw through economic disparity but to his former gang, who Marston will now pursue in the "less kind way," as he puts it. While corporate and government interests are to blame for the various fractures in property in New Austin and in turn, losses suffered by NPCs this suffering is displaced by Marston's role as a bounty hunter and lawman. That is, property crimes are enacted by rustlers and outlaws who must come to justice, which depoliticizes the suffering of, for example, the MacFarlanes.

Upon leaving the MacFarlanes', Marston joins Marshal Johnson on a number of missions that are designed to repair the fractures to private property while recognizing the overall importance of corporate interests. One mission in particular highlights the ways neoliberalism manages to depoliticize the suffering of those who are clearly harmed by corporate greed while sustaining hierarchies of identity that privilege rugged white masculinity. In the first mission, Marston and the marshal have a discussion that maps out the relationship between the marshal and his employers. The scene opens with the marshal answering a telephone, a signifier of civilization that connects the marshal to his employer, the railway company. The marshal cannot figure out how to use this newfangled technology and hangs up, saying to Marston, "If it's important, they'll send someone down to take care of it, like they did with you." Marston replies, "Suddenly, the world is full of 'theys.'" This exchange locates Marston and the marshal as company men, yet they are clearly representative of rugged masculinity. Further, Marston notes an important shift in terms of where power is located: no longer the domain of religion and other forms of local authority, "the world is full of 'theys'"—the nameless, faceless corporations that govern the lives of the characters in *Red Dead Redemption* (and, likely, its players).

In the middle of the conversation, Eli—an overweight, bucktooth, lazy-eyed deputy who represents a failed version of the rugged frontier hero—interrupts and frantically announces that the Bollard twins "and a couple of Mexicans" were seen stealing "Mr. Gulch's livestock." From there, the cutscene ends and gameplay begins as Marston, the marshal, and his intellectually deficient deputies ride to Pike's Basin to deal with the rustlers. One of the features of Rockstar's open-world games is the dialogue that occurs while the player travels from one mission to the next. In this case, MacFarlane's complaints about government corruption are reiterated, but the marshal resigns himself to the inevitability of domination by government, corporate interests, and rapid technological change:

> MARSHAL: I ain't for all this government interference.
> MARSTON: Believe me, Marshal, neither am I.
> MARSHAL: I try to keep the federal boys happy. I mean we need all the help we can get, but what does a city-boy, who's never forked a bale of hay in his life, know about a state like New Austin?
> DEPUTY: Nothin' I reckon.
> MARSHAL: All this Manifest Destiny hogwash. Tamin' a wild land; bringin' modernization and betterments to the West. It's only made the rich, richer and the poor, poorer and it's killed a way of life.

Once the marshal and Marston reach Pike's Basin, they kill all the rustlers upon whose shoulders rests the fault for ruptures in ownership and property. The "interference" by government and corporate interests that the marshal bitterly complains of becomes part of the discursive landscape, along with the cacti, and does not produce political resistance and action. The status quo, no matter how reviled, remains.

Eventually, however, players meet with the government agent from the Bureau of Investigation, Edgar Ross, who put Marston on the train to New Austin in the opening cutscene. Ross is an embodiment of modernity who drives a motorcar and shoots automatic weapons, and he would seem to be the figure of neoliberal oppression, but he is not. As a lone individual whose mantra is "everyone pays for what they have done," Ross is able to displace responsibility for Marston's death and the deaths or suffering of other characters through empty platitudes that encode the ideals of suffering and corporate capitalism. No one is sure who will pay whom, but Ross as the repressive agent of ideological state apparatuses will ensure that payment is made in full. Those who live in New Austin must bear "all the weight of the suffering produced by capitalism," which means by extension that most U.S. citizens, except the owners of the means of production, must also bear this weight as well.[50]

I admit I have presented a rather negative portrayal of *Red Dead Redemption*'s diegesis, which is composed of a mainly white, masculine, individualistic, free-market, heteronormative world that resuscitates Wister's "*eternal inequality*." Perhaps there are cultural and social benefits to working through a game world and figuring out the narrative paths that will lead to greater glory and profit. I am more hopeful that game publishers and corporations might consider other forms of the Western genre that aren't prone to deploying harmful belief systems, such as white supremacy. Even better, perhaps higher education, particularly the humanities, can do a better job of addressing the cultural, political, and social implications of game worlds.

2 Manifest Memory

The Role of Mexico in *Red Dead Redemption*

Stories of all kinds are often classified as entertainment, which is a gross misrepresentation of the power stories have to heal or poison. Laguna Pueblo writer Leslie Marmon Silko's poem about the power of story succinctly defines why we need to care about game stories:

> They aren't just entertainment
> Don't be fooled.
>
> They are all we have, you see,
> All we have to fight off illness and death.
> You don't have anything
> If you don't have the stories[1]

While Silko is referring to Laguna Pueblo stories, there is a lesson here that stories make our worlds plausible, real, and even aspirational. Stories are the primary means through which we think, fantasize, and behave—theorists from Mieke Bal to Marie-Laure Ryan have made it clear that stories, as Silko says, are not simply entertainment. In gameplay, the power of story can be amplified, particularly if genre conventions control and direct gameplay. To explain by way of comparison, in the print version of the frontier club Western, the reader has more distance from the story, whereas in most video games social interactions and behaviors are enacted and expressed by the player.[2] That is, gameplay is performative, requiring the player to take on a role or multiple roles in a game world. But what if those roles are racist, sustaining white supremacist ideals? *Red Dead Redemption* enables the conditions through which players can enact such values and beliefs.

Making White Supremacy Playable

Once players have completed the missions in New Austin, they then head to a fantastical province located in Mexico, which the developers Christian Cantamessa, Leslie Benzes, and head writer Dan Houser sardonically named Nuevo Paraiso (New Paradise). The Mexico missions revive (or perhaps feed into) the hackneyed stereotype that Mexico and its citizens are uncivilized, poverty stricken, and in need of law and order.[3] From the malnourished horses that stand in stark contrast to the robust beasts in New Austin to wild gunfights breaking out on the road (bullets zing by Marston's head from time to time while traveling between missions), this game-world Western furthers the stereotypical worldview that Mexico is a chaotic mess filled with degenerate species. In the style true to the frontier Western and borderlands narratives, players are transported not just "from one country to another, but one national system of classification to another."[4] In *Red Dead Redemption*, players travel, through the main character John Marston's perspective, as ethnographic explorers into a morally and historically bankrupt version of Mexico during the Mexican Revolution. But why replicate this period of Mexican history? Why embroil Marston in this particular political battle?

The answer is complicated. Mexican history, politics, and culture have served as a consistent narrative means to define white American identity as superior. Throughout the Mexico missions, Marston is positioned as the rational American surrounded by chaos. His status is bolstered by his love of family and desire to return to his homestead. One of the defining characteristics of being a successful American citizen is homeownership.[5] In chapter 1, I described Marston as a dedicated and responsible homeowner (he even has to complete chores on his property during one set of missions). The developers could have made him a lone gunslinger, but Marston's status as father and homeowner render him a prototype of a middle-class American. That is, the frontier myth, perpetuated by the frontier club Western, asserts that hardy and rugged settlers (property owners) must suffer to build the right kind of American character. The loss of property and status is not something to complain about or blame on systemic social and economic problems; rather, good Americans pull themselves up by their bootstraps. This philosophy, expounded most famously by President Teddy Roosevelt, a member of what Christine Bold calls the "frontier club," is a major ideological engine of the frontier Western.[6] In one of Roosevelt's most famous speeches, "The Strenuous Life," he championed the war-like and independent qualities of the American male, who is uplifted by fighting and struggle but weakened by "over-civilization."[7] Marston has to fight continuous battles to keep his property, a message to players that homeownership and family are not for the faint of heart. Put another way, economic downturns are not the fault of unfettered capitalism but by a populace weakened by "over-civilization."

Red Dead Redemption tries to persuade players that painful, violent struggle is part and parcel of being American. Marston has to fight to get back to his family and homestead, and even then, he loses everything. Victoria Lamont explains that struggle over class and property are defining elements of the Western such as in Wister's *The Virginian* (1902), B. M. Bower's *The Happy Family* (1910), Frances McElrath's *The Rustler* (1902), and even Jane Smiley's *A Thousand Acres* (1991), to name a few.[8] Of course, these novels influenced films that also remediate this class struggle, such as *The Virginian* (Stuart Gilmore's film in 1946 and the subsequent television show, which ran from 1962 to 1971). The Western has furthered the ends of the frontier myth, which defines land as the means to build and sustain American character: property is not for "savages" but for hardy (white) homesteaders who can suffer and struggle to prove the land. Is it any wonder that the Western has seen a resurgence since the economic collapse? From television shows like *Fear the Walking Dead* (a zombie Western that first aired in 2015) to games like Ubisoft's *Gunslinger* (2013), the Western (particularly frontier Westerns) make the struggle of the American middle class not only palatable but an apparent necessity to being a strong American citizen.[9]

Literary genres respond to the zeitgeist. *Red Dead Redemption*, as a frontier Western, addresses the ongoing crisis of a declining middle class. As of 2018 the U.S. housing and mortgage industry—the lifeblood of the American Dream—is still recovering from the 2008 collapse. The housing market in several key areas in the United States has not bounced back; in Tampa, Florida, "thousands of homes have been lost to foreclosure in the past decade."[10] The Pew Research Center released a report in 2017 that revealed the American middle class has shrunk over the last two decades "compared with those in many Western European countries."[11] Increasing numbers of Americans, particularly black and Latinx citizens, are finding it harder to participate in the culture of property ownership and accumulation that has traditionally defined American success and dominance over other countries.[12]

Marston's journey through Mexico counters the fact of middle-class decline through comparison with the degradation he encounters. *Red Dead Redemption* continues a long-standing tradition in American storytelling to define the Mexican Revolution as a frontier Western. Mark Anderson explains that the frontier Western (meaning a Western that fully embraces the frontier myth) typically triumphs archetypal masculine Americana (bravery, whiteness, self-control) while casting primarily Mexicans and "Indians" as dishonest savages with no self-control.[13] The Mexico missions follow this generic pattern to a tee while exemplifying American middle-class values (property ownership, family obligation, monogamy, and self-control) as paramount via Marston's example.

The Mexico missions redefine the American middle class not only as stable and desirable but also as under threat unless protected from apparent teeming masses south of the border. The frontier Western defines the American West as a series of "white enclaves reserved for superior species,

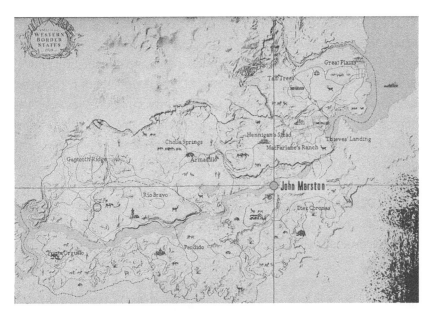

3. MAP BORDER. *RED DEAD REDEMPTION.*

animal or human, fringed and threatened by degenerate species."[14] That is, the patrician members of the frontier club often referred to immigrants in their stories as animals that need to be removed from the U.S. environment to protect its interests. A game-world Western like *Red Dead Redemption* provides "proof" for Trump's rants about Mexican immigrants.[15] With this concept of Latinx immigrants as "degenerate species" in mind, the following discusses how gameplay and its affordances create a playable white triumphalist experience.

The Affordances of Whiteness

The player is repeatedly reminded of their position on one side of the border or the other through the necessity of viewing the game map in order to progress. The map requires the player to exit gameplay by pressing the Start button and choosing the map from a list of functions in the main menu. While this action might seem to interrupt gameplay, it is a digital affordance that "make[s] possible—and, in some cases, [is] used to encourage—certain types of practices."[16]

The map requires players to leave the diegetic space of the game and enter into a 2-D view of the 3-D world the player once occupied. The player is situated in the game narrative through a multimodal menu, bathed in the conventional red and sepia tones of the spaghetti Western. This retro reference to the spaghetti Western taps into "the emotional residue" left behind by a "larger narrative economy." That is, explains Henry Jenkins, game developers "draw upon [players'] previously existing narrative competencies," and while this assertion is astute, Jenkins does not connect the ideological and social implications of genre to these narrative competencies.[17] The game map is an ideological affordance, which positions Marston as part of a "real" historical setting: he is a witness to Mexican degradation of democratic and capitalist values, which means, by extension, the player is as well.

Players cannot fully resist or leverage the affordance (unless they stop playing the game) but must press the "map" button and be transported into the bird's-eye view of a worn, yellowed print map.[18] The map ensures that the player is almost always within sight of the much larger and imposing New Austin (the American West), which is positioned above Nuevo Paraiso; therefore, the player must *descend* into Mexico from the heights of the New Austin landscape. This virtual geographical hierarchy is not simply replicated in map form but in gameplay; the player, as Marston, must ride down a steep embankment to the San Luis River, where—like a frontier club hunter—Marston must cull the landscape of "degenerate species" in order to progress in the game.

What I'm getting at here is that the game's geography is significant; after all, developers could have started the game in a replica of Wyoming and then simply transported the player through a kind of ludo-ellipsis to Mexico. Instead, players have to consistently refer to the map in order to find locations and missions. If a player has absolutely no interest in gameplay and drifts through the game's geography, then the map is insignificant, but if a player wants to complete any missions, then the map must be consulted frequently. Maps are not representations of truth but create a spatial concept of whatever is being represented.[19] In other words, maps tell a story from a certain worldview. The map in *Red Dead Redemption* tells the player that

New Austin is the center area between Nuevo Paraiso and Tall Trees and Great Plains (both located within the larger territory of West Elizabeth, adjacent to New Austin), where "Indians" live. In a sense, New Austin and West Elizabeth operate as Eurocentric mediating forces between two "outlaw breed[s]," the Mexican and the Indian.[20] Because this frontier Western has been promoted as a "historically accurate" video game, the map seems real and reinforces a classification system where "civilization" (but not "over-civilization" aka intellectualism) is far superior to the degradation just below its borders.[21]

The game reiterates an exceptionalist compulsion to position the United States as "the fulfillment of the national ideal to which other nations aspire."[22] John Mason Hart explains that "from the beginnings of the nineteenth century to the present, the citizens of the United States attempted to export their unique 'American Dream' to Mexico," which includes social mobility, free-market capitalism, and consumer culture.[23] Few theorists have put more work into understanding the West as a mythic spatial concept than Richard Slotkin, who explains that "mythic symbols encode paradigms or programs of real-world action, drawn from past experience or historical memory, which are projected as hypothesis about the outcomes of prospective action."[24] One of Slotkin's few drawbacks as a historian is that he makes these exciting proclamations but then undercuts his own argument by largely neglecting the fact that such "interpretive models" are not scientific or empirical but support ideological imperatives. When Slotkin states that mythic symbols encode the paradigmatic myths that make the world understandable and safe for certain citizens, it's logical to assume that not all of these myths provide "interpretive models" that work positively or even safely for others who belong to marginalized and underrepresented cultural groups.

Red Dead Redemption casts Mexican citizens and government as failures at nation-building. Philip Pendix-Tadsen argues that even though the Mexican characters in *Red Dead Redemption* "are off center and not entirely likable, this puts them on a level playing field with all the game's characters who are all driven by self-interested desires and motivations."[25] Certainly, there are a number of unlikable characters, such as the necrophiliac Seth Briars, but it's hard to imagine more likable characters than Bonnie MacFarlane and her father, the marshal, or Landon Ricketts, who are all stock characters drawn from the frontier Western: Bonnie is the well-educated woman forced to learn the ways of the West; her father is the classic small rancher, trying to do right by his family; the marshal is the rugged yet beleaguered law man, who protects his community; and Ricketts is a former gunslinger who protects the good citizens of Chuparosa.

By contrast, characters such as Abraham Reyes, the rebel leader, are more than simply "off-center"; Reyes is represented as a megalomaniac sex addict. I don't think it's logical or productive to conduct a one-to-one comparison of Reyes to the major rebel leaders of the revolution, such as Francisco Madero and Pancho Villa; however, an analysis of Reyes as a character reveals a great deal about how *Red Dead Redemption* revises Mexican history. In the introduction, I noted that video game critic Harold Goldberg heralded the historical accuracy of *Red Dead Redemption*, which speaks to the illusion game-world Westerns can create.[26] Video games as a form of popular entertainment can operate much like propaganda, furthering ideological concerns for specific, often privileged, populations. Video games like *Red Dead Redemption* are not simply entertainment, but like all popular culture, are "inflected by power and politics."[27] Abraham Reyes, among other characters, is a deeply political figure who works in service to white supremacist, exceptionalist ideologies.

I wish I could say that Reyes is an isolated case, but all the Mexican leaders in the game, regardless of political stripe, are portrayed as drunken or promiscuous power-hungry cretins. The only character with any saving grace is Luisa Fortuna, a former teacher and rebel who is madly in love with Reyes. He cares nothing for her, which makes him an unreliable and morally degraded character, and she seems to lack insight since Reyes is a known womanizer. Each of these representations play into common stereotypes of Mexican identity circulated by the Hollywood Western, particularly the "Mexico westerns" of the 1940s and 1950s, when the Eisenhower administration "was developing a policy scenario for American engagement in the Third World," Hollywood responded with Westerns that addressed "the same ideological concerns."[28] *Red Dead Redemption* remixes these "ideological concerns" into an interactive, playable environment, rendering Mexico and its inhabitants as immoral, chaotic, hysterical, and debauched. In other words, Mexico needs intervention from heroes like John Marston and Landon Ricketts, replicating the dominant mode of American foreign policy to intervene whether a nation wants help or not.

What is really at stake when games like *Red Dead Redemption* represent Mexico as a backward, morally corrupt nation? Such games are part of a state of fantasy that enable Americans—such as President Donald Trump and his followers—to make outrageous statements about Chicana/Chicano identity and culture and, more problematically, feed into the systemic racism that the larger Latinx community suffers on a daily basis. Further, these games, such as Techland's *Call of Juarez* series (particularly *The Cartel*), counter Latinx power.[29] Actually, there aren't many games that represent Latinx identity in an explicitly positive manner or even as playable characters. Latinx characters are most often nonplayer characters, which are characters powered by scripted behaviors rather than being embodied by the player. Such games are not simply "racist" but build the cultural capital of white (particularly male) Americans through opposition and negation. Latinx identity is expressed as expendable in order to further the myth of white triumphalism when the truth is that the white population in the United States is actually in decline.

The Latinx community in the United States has grown in the last two decades, with "one in six Americans now Hispanic." This shift in U.S. demographics means that "Hispanics are transforming the definition of what it means to be American" and also signaling a "white decline."[30] This "white decline" is not simply about demographics but about social, economic, and political control. U.S. politicians, with Trump as one of the most vocal and media savvy, can make false claims about Latinx people such as that they (and black Americans) are responsible for most violent crime because cultural narratives such as the frontier Western tell white Americans that they have the right to make ethnographic, simplistic, and incorrect claims about nonwhite U.S. citizens. The belief that one has the right to make such claims is part of exceptionalist state fantasy, explains Donald Pease, whereby the very idea of race is effaced through "disowning the knowledge of the historical realities of imported slave labor, of overseas colonialism, and of the economic exploitation of refugees."[31] It's also part and parcel of Western cultural practice to believe that all forms of cultural praxis is available for use by anyone, including in video games.[32] The struggles of "Asian, Hispanic, and American Indian groups for recognition of their equal rights" exposes American exceptionalism as primarily a discourse of whiteness.[33] The lack of a playable Mexican characters, the buffoonery of the Mexican characters, and even the setting speak to this fact. *Red Dead Redemption* follows the convention of featuring Latinx characters as merely "obstacles to overcome" and not fully realized characters.[34] The game missions exemplify this convention.

The Missions

The Mexico missions are organized into two main political factions that the player must deal with: the ruling faction of Colonel Agustin Allende and Captain Vincente de Santa and the rebel faction represented by the leader Abraham Reyes and his partner Luisa Fortuna. Most missions feature women being captured and sexually assaulted, extreme violence, drunkenness (and accompanying buffoonery), and corruption on both sides. Marston does not take sides but operates as a type of double agent to get what he wants: the fugitives Javier Escuella and Bill Williamson. Marston, of course, helps those who need it but peppers his interactions with criticisms of the country, its government, and citizens. Imagine if these missions gave players the option to play as, for example, Pancho Villa or Francisco Madera, and not as caricatures? The game narrative would have been made more complex and multifaceted, not to mention ethical.

The first mission features Marston entering Mexico via the San Luis River. Led by the drunken criminal Irish (the embodiment of another stereotyped ethnicity in the game), Marston crosses what is clearly the Rio Grande (which divides Mexico and Texas), despite the name change. He slaughters the attacking banditos, who are after Irish for his indiscretions in Nuevo Paraiso. While the player is well aware that Marston has an apparently good reason for killing masses of banditos (he is trying to save his family), it's ethically necessary to ask the point of this slaughter. Why does it occur on this replication of the Rio Grande rather than in Mexico or New Austin? While it's true that the recessed river with its ledges and peaks makes for exciting gun play, these kinds of peaks and valleys to duck behind and shoot enemies are also available in the southwestern territories of Nuevo Paraiso and New Austin. Therefore, the choice to have Marston battle his way into Nuevo Paraiso via the San Luis River (aka the Rio Grande) is as significant as the narrative action and gameplay that occurs in this borderland.

The Rio Grande/San Luis River mission resembles John Ford Westerns, in which the Rio Grande is a "fixed and perilous border, the home or refuge of savages."[35] Jim Kitses explains that Westerns—and I argue the frontier Western in particular—dress up the white male as "the embodiment of America's Manifest Destiny." Ford helped to institute this embodiment, most often via John Wayne, furthering the racial and sexual dynamics of the Western in which the Indian, the Mexican, and the white woman are "constructed as archetypal agents that define the hero's direction." The viciousness and violence of the Mexican banditos stand in stark contrast to the cowboy hero Marston, who is characterized as the victim, forced to defend himself from an overwhelming number of banditos. In Nuevo Paraiso (aka northern Mexico) Marston is the classic Ford hero, acting not for himself but for duty and honor.[36] If you need more convincing, there is an actual "honor bar" that appears at the bottom of the screen after Marston completes a mission and that increases or decreases depending on Marston's/the player's choice to shoot an innocent bystander or save a victim. Therefore, the game is designed to urge players to behave as a classic cowboy hero à la Ford or Wister's models of rugged masculinity. Yet part of this honorable behavior is to shoot banditos (I killed well over a hundred). These massacres beg the question: why is Marston considered civilized, particularly when compared to de Santa or Allende? Because de Santa and Allende are presented as dangerous predators that need to be put down.

In the de Santa missions, players are introduced to Captain Vincente de Santa, and in the first cutscene the player witnesses de Santa delicately stroke the face of a teenage boy. Captain de Santa is the only character in the game who is apparently gay; this is confirmed later in the game. In one of the final missions involving the military leaders, and after de Santa is murdered, one of the soldiers says, "A lot of young men will sleep better in their beds," casting de Santa as a sexual predator. This game world seems to perpetuate a dangerous stereotype that gay men are sexual predators. Captain de Santa is a vile character who has no redeeming qualities, and neither does his superior officer, Colonel Allende.

In a sense, de Santa and Allende are doubles, both perpetuating the myth that Latinx men are sexual predators. Where de Santa apparently rapes teenage boys, Allende rapes young women. These actions are reinforced by a convention of gameplay that Patrick Jagoda calls "punitive ethos," in which players must replay levels of the game until the win-lose conditions have been successfully met.[37] Therefore, players may well be exposed repeatedly to de Santa's and Allende's sexual and political crimes, reinforcing stereotypes. Players can skip missions in *Red Dead Redemption*, presumably to ensure the continuity of the game narrative, but by doing so they risk losing valuable fame and honor points. As David Golumbia argues, players should consider who they are killing in video games and why. Marston may be a classic Western hero, but he kills "not for some sense of the 'greater good' but because those one kills are understood to be 'less than' oneself."[38] This representation of violence is common in stereotypical border narratives, explains Camilla Fojas, and have been in production "since the inception of cinema . . . [which] has commandeered the borderlands to tell a story about U.S. dominance in the American hemisphere." The border is a contested space that has been represented in print and film, but in a game world, the encoding of the border adds the element of performativity, asking players to enact these ideologies. Fojas's assertion that the southern border is a trope that "capture[s] a range of 'American' ideals and rugged survivalism, confidence, and self-sufficiency" describes the frontier mythos of Marston's journey into Mexico.[39] He may be saving his family, but his mission has a high body count of degenerate individuals because the ends justify the means in this exceptionalist landscape.

It's impossible to discuss all the missions in this section of the game (it took me at least eight hours to complete all the missions and side missions), but as Landon Ricketts is a character that certainly helps to define and highlight white privilege in the game, I need to include him in the chapter. Ricketts is a broken-down gunslinger who left New Austin for Mexico. Both Marston and Ricketts operate as a form of law enforcement, helping only those who deserve to live, such as Luisa Fortuna, who Ricketts describes as "a human being, not like others here." As a former cowboy-outlaw, Ricketts has the ethos and racial markers to bestow humanity on some but dehumanize others based on an ambiguous value system. The cutscenes and missions with Ricketts define the border between Nuevo Paraiso and New Austin as more than a separation between settings, but an existential division that characterizes Ricketts and Marston as saviors (they are literally called "saviors" by those they help in Chuparosa). Ricketts describes he and Marston as "low rent messiahs." Even though Ricketts makes this statement sarcastically, the meaning is clear: he and Marston are exceptional individuals in a foreign land that apparently needs saving. Marston and Ricketts enable players to perform the stereotypical function of the borderlands to "manage traumatic and undesirable histories and ultimately reaffirm core 'American' values."[40] They are the embodiment of American exceptionalist foreign policy.

This procedural replication of northern Mexico circa 1911 detaches history from its "double reference to the past and to the real," explains Claudio Fogu, who claims that digital representation of history, such as in complex video games, is changing how players understand history as a representation of what *happened* to what *might be*. That is, as players progress through a historical event, they are less worried that the game accurately represents historical events and more worried about what will happen in the game.[41] When Ricketts revises Mexican history by explaining to Marston that Mexico has been a hotbed for revolution since the Spanish left, it's highly unlikely the player will check facts. Brian Rejack argues that historically based games are akin to historical reenactment, which tells us more about the present than the past.[42] History becomes a visceral performance based in immediacy rather than a critical, detached reflection of what came before. *Red Dead Redemption*, then, is not about history but about the position of the United States in the twenty-first-century global landscape. As Jason Dittmer makes clear, popular culture is a hotbed of political debate, and *Red Dead Redemption* has the reach to influence how players understand Mexico as a geopolitical entity.

The Ricketts missions exemplify the goals of U.S. foreign policies in the twentieth and twenty-first centuries, which are to ostensibly save the foreign other from perceived calamity. Ricketts's dismissal of the Mexican people, in whose country he lives, is indicative of the cultural superiority endemic not only to the Western but the United States at large. In general, white Americans have a belief in "personal superiority over Mexicans . . . blended with an indifference that allows corporate interests to do what they please in Mexico."[43] Ricketts's comment that he and Marston are "low rent messiahs" position them as the second coming of righteousness, and low rent or not, their cultural and racial superiority are made clear.

Marston's purpose in Nuevo Paraiso is to track down his former gang member Javier Escuella, who is given little backstory in the game. Wearing a sombrero and bandoliers, he looks the part of the Mexican villain. This style of villain came to prominence in the United States during the Mexican Revolution, which, Juan Alonzo tells us, "changed everything." The revolution changed the way Mexican identity was portrayed in American film, spawning the bandito. The successful revolt of the Mexican peasants against the upper classes was supported by left-leaning American intelligentsia and "progressive writers," who "championed the potentially liberating social movement in Mexico." However, Hollywood did not take this progressive view, and the Mexican revolutionary became an easy enemy to reproduce in film.[44] Furthermore, the Mexican bandito in a twenty-first-century video game reminds all players of every nationality where lawlessness resides: Mexico. From the vigilantism of the Minutemen who guard the U.S.-Mexico border to the racist claims made by primarily populist politicians about Mexico, *Red Dead Redemption* reinforces stereotypes and reassures white Americans that while their superiority is assured, it must be vigilantly protected. Escuella is ostensibly a gang member, dressed as the classic Mexican villain; he embodies the fear that Latinx criminals will invade the United States and bring chaos.

Indeed, the bandito was created to perform just this kind of cultural work. *Red Dead Redemption* anachronistically articulates early twentieth-century values, echoing Randolph Hearst (whose property was under threat by the revolution), who claimed that to "impress the Mexicans is to REPRESS the Mexicans."[45] As the frontiersman figure, Marston creates order out of chaos, quelling anxieties that the United States is no longer a superpower that brings civilization to the beleaguered masses. By casting Latinx and Mexican Americans as "savages," the games tries to persuade the player that Latinx peoples will not become the dominant force for political and social change in the United States.

In order to get to Escuela, Marston must first befriend the leader of the revolution, Abraham Reyes, who is an amalgam of various revolutionaries, including Francisco Madero, Pancho Villa, and Emiliano Zapata, with his handlebar mustache and goatee and rebel garb. Players cannot avoid the Reyes missions in the game, or they are punitively blocked from capturing Escuela. The procedural rhetoric of the game demands that players fulfill a certain number of missions, each of which builds the argument that Mexican leaders are degenerate. Reyes's lust for women and power is replicated in the form of military and government leaders who Marston must spend time with before meeting with Reyes. Colonel Allende is a drunk who forces Marston to join him in a wholesale slaughter of a village, save for the women, who are rounded up for Allende. This form of state violence is set in stark contrast to Allende's American double and Marston's nemesis, Agent Edgar Ross of the Bureau of Investigation, who is also violent and intrusive but mainly operates quietly behind the scenes. Edgar Ross surveils the populace, ensuring the rights of corporations to make a profit, but he does not round up women or vomit in front of Marston, as Allende does. So what is the procedural and narrative argument here? What are players persuaded of?

Allende and Ross are related in their use of power to further corruption and their own positions, but Allende is rendered a poor copy of Ross's exceptionalist and chilling code of honor where "everyone must pay." Homi Bhabha theorizes that mimicry is a powerful colonial tool where the colonized other is depicted as nearly the same but not quite the same as the colonizer.[46] In other words, Allende is a buffoonish parody. Allende's abject antics and sexual promiscuity contrast Ross's mysterious yet all-American presence as a pathologically patriotic man who also enjoys duck hunting. Again, the border between Nuevo Paraiso is not simply geographical but neocolonial, reinforcing Mexican identity as the poor, abject cousin. The player's time in Allende's camp comes to an end when he cannot deliver Escuella to Marston.

Upon leaving Allende, Marston runs into the hapless Luisa Fortuna, who is in love with Reyes. She informs Marston that Reyes has been captured by government forces, and in order to further his own ends, Marston agrees to help. Fortuna responds, "Oh, Mr. Marston, you truly are a friend to this land." He sarcastically retorts, "So everyone keeps informing me," echoing the indifference with which Mexican politics is met by much of the American populace.[47] Fortuna's name is ironic since she is one of the more tragic characters. She is doubly deceived, as Reyes tells Marston that he does not love Fortuna but "enjoyed" her for a while. In both cases, Fortuna lacks power and influence despite her bravery. Mexican women, like all other women in this game, do not fare well. Fortuna's counterpart is Bonnie MacFarlane, the ranch owner. It's MacFarlane who nurses Marston back to health and pays him to work as a ranch hand. (White) women are needed in Westerns to help the male hero recuperate. She is at once a reminder of the civilization he must return to and "a midwife . . . who ensures through a feminine presence . . . that masculine restraint will be restored."[48] However, Luisa does not serve the recuperative function Bonnie MacFarlane does but is instead a handmaiden to Marston's mission and a tragicomic figure through her unrequited love for Reyes. When Marston finally rescues Reyes, players discover that he is no better than Allende. He, like Allende, abuses his authority both politically and sexually.

There is no clear difference between the corrupt governmental/military figures and the corrupt revolutionary figures. The doubling of the revolutionaries and the government furthers the game's argument that resistance is futile. This argument is made clear through an exchange between Marston and Fortuna. Marston asks Fortuna why her own people treat each other "like shit." Fortuna responds that the Mexicans "are the same as the Americans. . . . We fought off the Spanish, we fought off the French, and we fought off the Americans. Finally, Mexico can defend itself and all we have done is fight each other." Marston surmises that revolution is useless because nothing ever changes. "We ain't ever free," he says.[49] Fortuna compares the Mexican Revolution to the American Revolution, a common

4. ABRAHAM REYES CHEATING ON LUISA FORTUNA. *RED DEAD REDEMPTION.*

association that Slotkin calls a "double-acting metaphor" in that the Mexican Revolution is compared favorably to the American Revolution but is also seen as a failure.[50] Again, Mexico is cast as the colonial other, a poor copy of the colonizer, always mimicking but unable to be a sovereign and successful nation.

Nowhere is Marston's moral superiority made more apparent than in the cutscene where Marston arrives at Reyes's for a meeting, only to find him on the dining room table, fucking one of his female followers. Before Reyes sees Marston, he screams "Viva Mexico!" at the top of his lungs, making the connection between his behavior and Mexican sovereignty quite clear. Mexico, to put it bluntly, is fucked.

Marston, without skipping a beat, asks Reyes to consider Fortuna's feelings; Reyes responds that he does not remember her. Marston reminds him that Fortuna thinks she is his wife. Reyes responds that peasant girls believe anything they are told and that he would never consider marrying a peasant because he will be president of Mexico one day. The reason he has sex with peasants, explains Reyes, is that he is trying to ensure that his aristocratic blood will flow into the peasant bloodline, improving the genetic and intellectual prospects of his people. This coital attempt at eugenics renders Reyes as more of a degenerate buffoon than presidential material, but that's the point, isn't it?

The Nuevo Paraiso missions changes the trajectory of Marston's character from a man beleaguered by neoliberal governmentality (but accepting that there is little he can do about it) to defining his cultural superiority via the chaos and buffoonery of his Mexican counterparts, which is not seen elsewhere in the game. Even in the Tall Trees and Great Plains missions, where Marston slaughters dozens of "Indians" (discussed in detail in chapter 3), Marston is not called upon to civilize the Indigenous characters, just exterminate them. Not so in Nuevo Paraiso, where the player bears witness to levels of corruption that are so hyperbolic as to render them nearly comic. While we witness corruption in New Austin via the federal government and corporations, the player does not see antagonists like Edgar Ross and Dutch van der Linde having sex with (or perhaps raping, it's unclear) women on dining room tables. The representation of the Mexican Revolution seems more like a gross parody of American corruption. This section of the game might be satire, but no authority is cut down or challenged. Rather, the borderlands that Marston traverses are a means to corroborate America's exceptionalism by affirming that America is the "Invincible Nation."[51]

Consider that historical games are experienced, not read or viewed, by players. That is, as Alison Landsberg asserts, "new cultural surfaces" that people interact with "affect people and shape their politics."[52] When players enter a game world, they are entering into performative structures of knowledge that profoundly impact their understanding of the world. Is there hope for a new way to imagine the borderlands in video games? Can the borderlands move beyond the entrenched visions of the border as teeming with "degenerate species," who must be segregated to stop any contagion? Thankfully, yes, indie game designers are trying to combat the pathological representations of Mexican and Latinx identity found so commonly in popular culture. Recently, Latino game designer and artist Gonzalo Alvarez developed an arcade-style game that simulates the dangers of the border crossing.[53] The game humanizes those seeking asylum by allowing players to simulate the experience of hiding from border guards, trying to find water, and generally avoiding the myriad of dangers at the border. While Alverez's game isn't a Western, his work offers a different perspective from the consistent white gaze that dominates most game worlds. Along these lines, the Western doesn't have to dehumanize, and the next chapter provides options for avoiding such representations in game-world Westerns.

3 Virtual Indian Removal

Why Indigenous Knowledge Matters in Game Development

Red Dead Redemption continues the convention of the frontier Western to define Indigenous identity as primitive, savage, underdeveloped, and vanishing. Settler society's perception of Indigenous peoples has been shaped by fictional narratives that are "degrading and offensive to most Indigenous Peoples for obvious reasons, and inaccurate in ways that still escape" North American authors, publishers, game writers, developers, players, and critics.[1] Game worlds are able to enact a form of ludo-colonization, explains Nick Dyer-Witheford and Greig de Peuter, because they support "systemic patterns of inequality and marginalization."[2] These patterns influence players because they "repeatedly enact, perform, and materialize a mode of being" that is mediated through the Western genre.[3] This performative remediation of history sustains and reinforces durable paradigmatic myths of colonization, such as white triumphalism and Indigenous inferiority. This chapter explores the ways the frontier Western and its forebears continue to shape the way settler society perceives Indigenous identity, culture, and sovereignty in game-world Westerns, with a specific focus on *Red Dead Redemption*.

The Colonial Work of Westerns

Westerns have a colonial genealogy that casts light on why anyone might find it acceptable to slaughter dozens of Indigenous characters in a video game. Westerns, and many types of frontier narratives, define Indigenous and non-Indigenous relations. The cultural work of the Western and its generic forebears has been in part to support policies of colonial domination, such as the Indian Removal and General Allotment Acts. This cultural work has been remediated in *Red Dead Redemption*, in which players are rewarded for violently removing almost all Indigenous nonplayer characters from the land—and quite literally, since a central mission is to shoot as many Indigenous NPCs as possible. Because "actual Indigenous people are judged as more or less authentic, more or less real, to the extent that they live up or down to a fictitious representation," the genres that underpin settler society perception of Indigenous identity need to be tracked and exposed for what they are: fallacious and poisonous.[4] By countering such representations, we can envision remedies for this ludo-colonization and perhaps even reenvision how game worlds can operate to decolonize rather than reenact colonial narratives.[5]

How did these representations become so embedded in the North American psyche? Part of the answer is through consistent repetition across hundreds of years. Paradigmatic myths of Indigenous identity, such as the "Noble Native" and the "Vanishing Indian," can be traced back to colonial contact with Indigenous peoples and the stories told by settler-colonists of this contact. The most popular of these stories were female captivity narratives, a durable genre that remains part of the North American cultural landscape.[6] As I explained in the introduction, the cultural and social implications of remediating durable genres into game worlds has been under-theorized, particularly considering that the repetition of the elements that comprise a genre induce social action. Genres help us to group symbols that in turn supply meaning and significance to various contexts and situations. A genre is a fusion of rhetorical forms bound together by an internal dynamic that provide guidelines for dealing with varied rhetorical situations.[7] So literary genres, particularly durable literary genres such as the captivity narrative and the Western, have an internal dynamic that is repeated, and through this repetition, readers both learn the formula of the genre and in turn gain knowledge from the formula that they can then apply when needed. As such, literary genres have influence on social situations by giving readers a repertoire to draw from.

The basic formula of the most enduring and popular captivity narratives involves a white woman who is captured by "bad Indians" from the safety of her home. Based on this formula, captivity narratives engineer relationships between race, colonization and patriotism, among other elements, and they continue to "demarcate legitimate and illegitimate identities" to this day.[8] Richard Slotkin examines how formulaic frontier narratives, such as the captivity narrative, are central to constructing a specifically American experience, reducing centuries of history and culture into a constellation of violent and destructive metaphors that define "national aspiration in terms of so many bears destroyed, so much land preempted, so many trees hacked down, so many Indians and Mexicans dead in the dust."[9] Via print and visual media over hundreds of years, the captivity narrative has spread diffusely across the American cultural field, becoming embedded in other literary and visual forms.

For example, the frontier romance, popular in the early to mid-nineteenth century, embraced the racial dichotomies of the captivity narrative, using the conventions of the white woman held captive by the male "savage" as a major plot point. The frontier hero who tries to save the captive, such as James Fenimore Cooper's protagonist Natty Bumppo (aka Hawkeye, Leatherstocking, La Longue Carabine, and Deerslayer) in his frontier pentalogy, was drawn from real-life national heroes such as Daniel Boone. Boone was popularized by land speculator (an early form of real estate agent) John Filson in *The Discovery, Settlement, and Current State of Kentucky* (1784) as the frontiersman who will protect "civilization" from "savage" forces. In both captivity and frontiersman narratives, the "Indian" is the central figure against which civilization can be defined, and this racialized caricature of Indigenous identity, in turn, became a central part of the frontier romance.[10] Cooper popularized the formula that would come to negatively define Indigenous identity through his 1826 best-selling frontier romance *The Last of the Mohicans*. Cooper unleashed two long-standing stereotypes of Indigenous identity in his novel, which justified aggressively controlling Indigenous culture and land: Chingachgook and Uncas, the friendly, noble Indian informants, and Magua, the savage and bad Indian, who must be killed to save civilization. This "Noble Native/Savage Indian" dichotomy had been set in place since first contact. John Smith's explorer narratives, which were bestsellers in the seventeenth century and beyond, trafficked these myths to a public hungry for salacious tales of New World savagery.

The plot of the frontier romance, which includes frontiersmen, captivity, violent rescue and retribution, "Noble" and "Savage" Indians, and a wilderness or frontier setting, was remediated into a booming dime-novel business that began in earnest in the mid-nineteenth century and continued into the early twentieth century. Dime novels furthered the tradition of the frontier romance to suture "nationhood to white male individualism and [reinforce] hierarchies of race and gender." While there were interventions by women, African Americans, and Indigenous authors, their texts could not compete with the rampant popularity of, for example, the *Deadwood Dick* series. The low-culture status of dime Westerns underwent a sea change in 1902 with the publication of Owen Wister's *The Virginian*. Wister and his frontier club changed the fortune of the Western as a form of cheap entertainment to an icon of American nationhood. As briefly discussed in chapter 1, a group of patrician easterners, including Teddy Roosevelt, George Bird Grinnell, Wister, and Henry Cabot Lodge, were part of Progressive Era club culture, in which business dealings, camaraderie, and ideological stances were shared by other well-heeled white men. This particular group of eastern aristocrats also belonged to the Boone and Crockett Club, founded by Roosevelt in 1887, and were largely responsible for the evolution of the modern Western: "The primary aim of the Boone and Crockett Club was lobbying for big-game hunting rights and conservation measures, activities for which they remain famous today. In 1893, however, they were also embarking on an authorial project, producing what would become a seven volume series—about ninety of the clubmen's hunting tales and essays in all . . . the most popular work emerging from the frontier club was Owen Wister's best-selling novel *The Virginian* published in 1902."[11]

This "frontier club"-driven Western, *The Virginian*, spawned movies and television shows and has never been out of print, in part because the clubmen who had a hand in creating *The Virginian* also had influence in the publishing world.[12] Authors wishing to counter the frontier club did not stand much of a chance against the wealth and influence of the clubmen. The ideological voice of these powerful men and their beliefs in rugged masculinity, passive women, frontier hardiness, and equal inequality also helped to define the caricature of the twentieth-century Indian. Wholly changing the "savage" Indian of the dime Western, Wister cleansed his Western of Indigenous presence, leaving only "a romantic residue of the past and a neutralized and fully contained component of the present, one doomed, according to popular thought, to vanish quickly." Wister's representation, of course, ignores encounters between Indigenous peoples and settler-colonists in the late nineteenth century, such as between tourists in the newly designated Yellowstone Park and the Nez Perce, who refused to be contained within the reservation system and fought their way across the American West into Canada. The tourists did not expect "vanishing Americans to reappear suddenly like Ghosts in war paint," and slaughter ensued.[13]

Moving into the twenty-first century, Dan Houser, co-founder of Rockstar Games as well as the head writer for *Red Dead Redemption*, continues the cultural work of the frontier club to render American cisgender, straight, white male identity and culture at the apex of the social order. Eerily reminiscent of the patrician easterners of the frontier club, Houser and his game developers understand themselves as possessing the privilege to erase the history of others. This all too brief genealogy of the frontier Western shows how erasure of Indigenous identity has become so engrained in the cultural landscape that slaughtering dozens of "Indians" in a frontier Western game world is deemed not only entertaining but necessary.[14] If genres such as the frontier Western have such a powerful influence, what happens when these genres frame not only a game's storyline but the procedures of gameplay that reward the player for performing the genre correctly? Let's see.

In the single-player game story option, Marston is the only character that can be embodied; therefore, he supplies the main spatial, psychological, and ideological perspective.[15] Ostensibly, Marston is the first-person narrator. He provides not only the controlling first-person perspective but a somatic and psychic self that is built, choreographed, and written into being through genre conventions that guide game processes and mechanics.[16] Similar to the Lacanian theory of the mirror stage, the player is "born into" the semiotics of the game, which encourages the player to think that they have control (via the controller), but in fact the 3-D image and cogito of John Marston—written into the procedural systems of game—are formed by the frontier Western, which influences the player. While the player has a certain amount of control over how the game story will be played, the semiotics of the frontier are laid out clearly, as are Marston's relationships with the racialized bodies in that space. That is (and as discussed earlier), the frontier Western was built to oppress. Players, therefore, are invited to use representations of indigeneity to encode their own sovereignty as opposed to recognizing that Indigenous peoples belong to sovereign, self-determining nations that have (or should have) power over their lands and resources: "The exertion of authority over Indigenous peoples and territories literally produces the foundation for the U.S. [and Canadian] state, and the interwoven forms of national belonging, property, and personhood that arise within the United States [and Canada] are marked by the ongoing inscription of settler sovereignty over Native polities and modes of place making."[17]

The codes of the frontier Western are encoded in *Red Dead Redemption*, which makes playable the "ongoing inscription of settler sovereignty over" Indigenous peoples through the Tall Trees and Great Plains missions of the game. There has been open condemnation of such representations of Indigenous culture, history, and identity by, for example, the Association for American Indian Development, which famously requested Activision recall its game *GUN* (2006). The game depicts Indigenous identity through the stereotype of the "savage warrior." Activision released a weak apology claiming that the company had no intentions of depicting Indigenous peoples negatively. The reaction from the internet tended to be condescending toward the request at best, implying that the misrepresentation of Indigenous identity is hardly an issue.[18] The Tall Trees and Great Plains missions are not only a foil against which American identity can claim indigeneity; it's also a violent reenactment of Indian removal that answers Louis Owens's question: Who gets to tell the story of the West?[19]

Virtual Indian Removal

Of course, Owens answers that question as clearly as *Red Dead Redemption* does: those who have wealth and privilege, more specifically those who have the financial and cultural capital to own a game system and feel at home in Marston's "skin," respectively. Similar to the representation of the frontier in *The Virginian*, the West is a space that contains only a residue of doomed Indigenous presence.[20] Tall Trees and Great Plains tell players that almost all of North America is a white space, cleared of "Indians," who have no future. It's not simply through killing dozens of "Indians" that this erasure is achieved. There are no Indigenous women in the Tall Trees encampment (that I could find); therefore, there can be no regeneration of Indigenous life and culture.

In a narrative move reminiscent of Cooper's *Last of the Mohicans*, *Red Dead Redemption* includes no Indigenous mothers. Set in juxtaposition to the threat of bloodthirsty savages in Tall Trees and Great Plains, the urban environment of Blackwater (in West Elizabeth, adjacent to Great Plains) is thriving, with symbols of progress at every turn, such as motorcars and movie theaters. However, this burgeoning urban world is under threat by "savages," who enter Blackwater to rob banks, cause mayhem, and, sometimes, kill white women. *Red Dead Redemption* suggests that the Indigenous population is not only hopelessly backward in comparison to white "civilization" but also barren. There can be no sovereignty for Indigenous peoples, no honoring of treaties and sharing of resources, because there is no Indigenous future in this game world. This version of the "Vanishing Indian" myth utterly removes any chance of Indigenous presence, but why does Indigenous culture need to be "vanished" in the twenty-first century?

Mark Rifkin explains that Indigenous sovereignty throws light on the "absence of an appropriate legal framework in which to consider the political issues and dynamics" at stake in Indigenous and non-Indigenous relations.[21] If Indigenous sovereignty is recognized, then non-Indigenous society will have to acknowledge and address exactly what Indigenous activists, scholars, and elected officials have been fighting for: honor the treaties and share resources. Indigenous sovereignty reveals the ruptures in claims of U.S. and Canadian multiculturalism and diversity by making its unethical and unjust (and even genocidal) practices plain. Therefore, Indigenous sovereignty must be removed from public discourse and rendered absent from the framework of public policy and knowledge. Frontier Westerns achieve this goal by creating a fantastical history of Indian removal and control. However, in the case of *Red Dead Redemption*, this game does more than circulate genocidal narratives; players are sutured to John Marston, taking up his subjectivity and therefore the ideological stance of the frontier Western.

In *Red Dead Redemption* and games like it, the rules of the game enforce a "root and branch" slaughter of marginalized others. That is, the procedural rhetoric of the game requires the player to either stop playing or continue by killing a vast number of "savages," who comprise not only Indigenous men but other disenfranchised NPCs, like the rustlers in New Austin, who resist the authority of the government. Clearly, the generic conventions of the frontier Western (and its progenitors) define the rules of this game world. The rules for gameplay in Tall Trees and Great Plains limit the player's choices, forcing the player to enact Indian removal violently, ensuring that Indigenous sovereignty and rights remain "vanished." I don't mean to suggest that Houser and his team of game developers knew what they were doing when they developed a frontier Western using powerful game mechanics. Game writers and developers likely envision the frontier Western genre as a means to make an exciting game in a recognizable story arc that will attract players (and a great deal of profit). Why did Houser and his developers have Marston slaughter masses of "Indians"? Because the dictates of the frontier Western demand the absent presence of "Indians."

Tall Trees is where Marston meets his most dangerous foe and former leader of his gang, Dutch van der Linde (who also appears in the prequel, *Red Dead Redemption 2*). Dutch has gathered a large number of disenfranchised "Indians" (of unknown tribal affiliation) who do not want to end up on

5. HAROLD MACDOUGAL AND NASTAS. *RED DEAD REDEMPTION.*

reservations. Of course, players don't actually know what they want because they say very little. Players only know what Dutch tells them. Conforming to the Hollywood stereotypes of "war paint and war bonnets" and "New Age" liberal movements, the "Indians" in *Red Dead Redemption* dance to the stereotypical choreography assigned to them by settler-colonist writers and developers.[22] However, before John Marston can meet with Dutch and his "Indian" henchmen, players meet with a Native Informant/Noble Native by the name of Nastas and a failed anthropologist, Harold MacDougal, who, like Marston, both work for former Pinkerton detective and member of the Bureau of Investigation, Agent Edgar Ross.

Mimicking the obedience of his narrative ancestors, Cooper's Chingachgook and Uncas, Nastas provides guidance and information about his people and laments their eventual demise. Harold is a ridiculous figure whose assumptions of Indigenous culture and "savagery" are unsuccessfully refuted by the stereotypically stoic Nastas.

Standing Rock Sioux scholar Vine Deloria famously described anthropology as a discipline that contributes "useless knowledge [by] attempting to capture real Indians in a network of theories[, which] has contributed substantially to the invisibility of Indian people today."[23] Similarly, Victoria Lamont explains that early twentieth-century ethnographers ironically created a market for stories by a people who would soon "vanish," apparently due to their inability to adapt to modern life, but this perceived cultural scarcity was actually caused by oppression of Indigenous peoples.[24] While Harold may be foolish, the presence of his Native Informant, Nastas, who talks about the inevitability of his people's doom, confirms Harold's ludicrous ideologies of indigeneity. In other words, it doesn't matter that MacDougal is a fool; he plans to publish his knowledge, while Nastas is forever silenced through his death. Therefore, in keeping with *Red Dead Redemption*'s general theme of political apathy in the face of injustice and inequality, the missions where Harold and Nastas debate suggest that it doesn't matter if Harold is incorrect: according to this game world, there are no "real Indians" left.

Perhaps even more disturbing than the ironic portrayal of Harold's view as fatally wrong yet the only one that will count is the fact that Nastas invites classic sentimentalism over the "vanishing" of his people. Indigenous peoples in the boundaries of the United States sit in a kind of limbo, according to Mark Rifkin, at once encompassed by U.S. law and excluded from it.[25] This complex paradigm of exclusion and erasure is mapped out in this game world. Similar to the figure of the "crying Indian" played famously by Italian American actor Iron Eyes Cody in an early 1970s commercial decrying the destruction of nature by urban progress, Nastas is a figure that laments "there is no respect for the land anymore." Nastas invites the player to share in sentimental feelings of loss over the Buffalo, the land, and his people, which flies in the face of thriving Indigenous cultures and movements across North America.

There are also interesting parallels between John Marston and Nastas. Both men sympathize with each other over loss. Similar to the conversations between the marshal and Marston over the encroachment of "civilization" in the New Austin missions, Marston and Nastas identify with the apparent loss each other suffers: Marston laments the loss of the "Old West" to urbanization, while Nastas laments the loss of his entire culture. However, neither fight the forces that are causing the loss, which are those who dominate and control the flow of information through education, like Harold,

6. MEMBERS OF DUTCH VAN DER LINDE'S GANG. *RED DEAD REDEMPTION.*

and the government that enforces laws and policies concerning who can have sovereignty and who cannot, like Edgar Ross. Marston and Nastas may reluctantly help Harold and Edgar stop Dutch and his gang of "Indians" and complain about it, but that is the extent of their resistance. While it is true that Marston has to follow Edgar's orders or his family's life is forfeit, why does Nastas follow the rules? Because the genre conventions of the frontier Western make clear that the Noble Native/Native Informant will always sacrifice his people.

I don't want to cast Dutch and his gang of "savages" as antiheroes, and players are also discouraged from casting them in this fashion for two reasons: 1) they kill Nastas, who Marston respects; and 2) the game rules demand that players kill every last one of them. Dutch's gang members are set in opposition to Nastas, keeping alive the nineteenth-century dichotomy popularized by Cooper between the Good Indians, who follow orders, and the Bad Indians, who take captives and resist. Indeed, Nastas is given a name, a history, and personality. This dichotomy is put into sharp relief when Nastas guides Marston and MacDougal to a meeting with Dutch's men. They are not given any depth and seem "savagely" angry, yelling at Marston, Nastas, and MacDougal to "LOOK AT US!" referring to the state of poverty they live in.

This meeting takes place in a dilapidated cabin, visually defining a state of disrepair and degradation. In fact, the entire setting cinematically narrates, on the one hand, poverty, with run-down buildings peppering the landscape, and, on the other, the stereotypical state of nature that represents the "authentic Indian" with wilderness as their home. Each of them are dressed in a blend of war paint and "Indian" costume, such as vests that have handprints on them and headbands; they each encode the markers of race with brown skin and angular faces. In other words, they meet the racial standards of the colonizers' gaze. The ensuing conversation casts Harold as the voice of reason:

HAROLD: Violence isn't the answer.

INDIAN: Maybe you live in a different America than we!

HAROLD: A man like van der Linde will lead you to disaster.

INDIAN: I think we have already experienced disaster, the likes of which you can only imagine.

Nastas tries to step in and make peace, but he's shot and killed, justifying Marston's subsequent slaughter of Dutch's men and, eventually, Dutch himself. In fact, if the player, as Marston, doesn't kill all the "Indians," then the mission fails, and there is no reward.

While it's true that missions can be skipped if the player continuously fails, failure means honor points and money are also lost, which makes working through the rest of the missions difficult. It's to the player's advantage to "beat" a mission, but let's consider what is being "beaten" here. The procedural rhetoric of this game world is dictated by the genre conventions of the frontier Western, part of which is to elide Indigenous presence. As David Brion Davis explains, "writers [of frontier narratives] had a certain justification for dwelling upon the ritual [of killing Indigenous peoples] since it signified the free white man's possession of the rights and privileges of his civilization, a racial eucharist, granting secular freedom and wealth after the sacrifice of a red man's flesh and blood."[26] *Red Dead Redemption* follows this historical precedent of sacrifice for the "greater good," but in this version of the frontier Western, players must slaughter dozens and dozens of Bad Indians to get to their leader: a cisgender, straight, white male who has been led astray by his belief in socialist ideals. Dutch at one time believed that taking from the rich and giving to the poor was a moral thing to do. Granted, this is not a ringing endorsement of socialism, but much like in the rest of the game, the government may be corrupt and the rich may get richer, but alternative forms of leadership, such as rustlers, Mexican revolutionaries, socialists (like Dutch), and Indian sympathizers (like Dutch), are not viable.

Empowering Indigenous Knowledge

What about a Western game world where Indigenous characters are developed based on principles of Indigenous systems of knowledge? How about game worlds where Indigenous developers play a role? Where a character like Nastas doesn't lament the fictitious loss of an entire people but embodies the thriving and vibrant Indigenous cultures of the present? How about Nastas is given an actual cultural affiliation, which he honors? Where Indigenous peoples do not need a white male to lead them? You might be thinking that the main player character from *Assassin's Creed III*, Ratonhnhaké:ton (aka Connor, the main character's adopted name), and his mother, Kaniehtí:io, fit the bill. If so, you are only partially right.

This game world is, as the title suggests, the third installment of the popular *Assassin's Creed* series. Ubisoft developers worked with Kanien'kehá:ka (Mohawk Nation) members to create respectful and responsible representations of Kanien'kehá:ka life and language. More specifically, developers consulted with Akwiratékha Martin, a teacher, and Teiowí:sonte Thomas Deer, a consultant, who both work at Kanien'kehá:ka Onkwawén:na Raotitióhkwa Language and Cultural Center.[27] The result is one of the more ethical representations of Indigenous peoples. Players embody Ratonhnhaké:ton as the main player character, completing missions from his childhood up into his indoctrination into the Assassin Brotherhood (a sacred group fighting the power-hungry Templar Order).

This all seems encouraging; however, as Anishinaabe scholar Niigaanwewidam Sinclair explains: "Gamers love—as much as most of pop culture—Indigenous representations. Indigenous peoples are the perfect toy to tell stories of land theft, war, and tragedy."[28] *Assassin's Creed III* is no different, with none other than George Washington giving the order to burn down Ratonhnhaké:ton's village. It's not simply that Ratonhnhaké:ton must tragically leave his people to save them from the Templars and along the way kill hundreds to reach his goals; he is also a paragon of rugged masculinity in that he is individualistic, competitive, and aggressive.[29]

The game mechanics often offer violence as the first choice when Ratonhnhaké:ton goes on one-man missions where he battles his way through, most of the time, solo. He may receive help along the way (such as from none other than Samuel Adams), but he is often the only one who can do what Adams or his mentor, Achilles, asks. Much like Marston, the player knows Ratonhnhaké:ton is the "alpha" character because he has such exceptional abilities compared to other men. Such inaccuracies and misrepresentations of indigeneity, such as Ratonhnhaké:ton's lack of humor and laughter (he is mostly the stoic Noble Native) could have been avoided if developers not only consulted but used resources by Indigenous developers, such as those by Métis developer Elizabeth LaPensée. Even better, game companies could hire Indigenous developers, so that video games can be "self-determining spaces, where Indigenous peoples can express themselves on their own terms."[30] *Assassin's Creed III* perpetuates the myth that rugged masculinity is a cross-cultural, conventional, and perhaps even natural means to make the man. Games that depend on the frontier myth and frontier Western narrative conventions invariably incorporate rugged masculinity; after all, that form of masculinity is the default in the majority of game worlds.

But this form of game and character development doesn't have to be conventional. I'd like to consider what such a game world might look like by using an example from a Western written by an Indigenous author: Mourning Dove's *Cogewea* (1927).[31] The eponymous hero of the game is Cogewea, a Syilx/Okanagan woman who is respected for her talents and skills by all of the cowboys on the ranch, most of whom are also Indigenous or multiracial. The antagonist is Alfred Densmore, who joins the ranch as an inept ranch hand. Densmore metaphorically represents Eurocentric colonization, which is known "among Indigenous peoples" as the "anti-trickster [who] represents the cognitive force of artificial European [and

American] thought . . . ever changing in its creativity to justify the oppression and domination of contemporary Indigenous peoples and their spirit guardians."[32] As the anti-trickster figure, Densmore is figuratively characterized as a serpent and more literally as a dangerous con artist who tries to steal Cogewea's property and money. Densmore seduces Cogewea into believing he loves her, but his actual intentions are sinister. He ends up taking Cogewea captive, but after he realizes she has little financial worth, he leaves her to die in the wilderness. We can already see that this Western has the potential to be remediated as an action game, but how would the mechanics work as part of the procedural rhetoric of the game? If games run on "procedural systems that generate behaviours based on rules based models," then what will these rules be?[33]

Drawing from Kenneth Burke's claim that we are symbol-using animals who are in turn influenced and driven by the symbols we use, Bogost theorizes that games are another form of persuasive symbol use. He stresses that part of the symbol-systems of a video game are computational procedures and rule-based systems, which means the unit operations of a game need to be analyzed and not simply the content or interface. To use drama as an analogy, the print text of a play provides little in the way of analytical material. The actual performance, with its staging, lighting, and other procedures, is just as important. This kind of analysis, particularly in literary and cultural studies where language and print have been fetishized, may seem rather alien, but it's a crucial aspect of any video game analysis.

That being said, Bogost does not seem to overtly consider that hundreds of years of "symbol-using" or storytelling conventions guide the procedural rhetoric of any game. As he states repeatedly, games make claims about the world, and in order for those claims to have cultural coherence, they must articulate the generic codes of that culture. Therefore, and to repeat the central thesis of this book, durable literary genres, like the Western, guide both the computational procedures and narrative framework of a game world. So let's return to our earlier question, now that the idea of procedural rhetoric is fresh in our minds: what will the procedural rhetoric of our Indigenous Western video game be? The chapter "Swa-Lah-Kin: The Frog Woman" in *Cogewea* contains a scene that would make for an interesting game experience. The setting of the chapter is a fishing expedition; Cogewea makes a bet with Densmore that he can't catch the first fish.[34] Densmore loses the first bet, then gambles five thousand dollars on the next cast, which he also loses. He doesn't pay either debt, of course. Cogewea playfully dismisses Densmore's actions, instead of seeing his behavior as a warning that Densmore does not keep his promises.

Not only does he not keep his promises, Densmore is greedy, desiring to catch more fish simply for sport, which causes Cogewea to scold him: "We have enough fish already. There are still a few left from yesterday's catch, and it is wrong and wasteful to hook them just for misconceived sport." Densmore ignores Cogewea, replying, "Wait a moment! I think there is a big shiner by that rock and I want him," which causes Cogewea to remind Densmore not to be selfish and to "leave a few for the next fellow who may really need them." This exchange, in effect, is a dialogue between two divergent epistemological systems: one is represented by Densmore as greedy, selfish, and consumerist, and the other is represented by Cogewea as sharing, land based, responsible and community oriented. These philosophies are central to Mourning Dove's Syilx/Okanagan knowledge system, which she expresses via *Cogewea*. The final offense involves Densmore toying with a small frog with his fishing pole, "mischievously [turning] it over and over towards her"; clearly, he expects a conventional sentimental female reaction, involving tears and recriminations. Instead, Cogewea patiently explains to Densmore that his actions with the frog will bring a violent storm, to which Densmore argues, "I supposed that you were enough educated to know better than to believe all those ridiculous signs of your people."[35] With these words, Densmore expects to trigger the cognitive imperialism instilled through her education at a residential school, which should cause her to dismiss her Syilx/Okanagan worldview and in turn respond within the conventional expectations for settler-colonist white female behavior. However, Cogewea will not conform to his expectations. Soon after the argument, a heavy rain starts to fall, proving Cogewea's story and discrediting Densmore even further.

The procedural rhetoric of a game version of this story could combine filmic sequences of Cogewea and Densmore heading to the river to fish with each character betting on who can catch the most fish. If the player, as Cogewea, loses the bet, then they also lose that particular part of the mission, replaying the act of catching trout until a certain number of fish remain. However, there must be a rule that if the player catches too many fish and keeps betting as Densmore, then they have not learned to avoid certain behaviors as explained by Syilx/Okanagan Elder and Canada Research Chair Dr. Jeannette Armstrong: "Offensive arrogant forwardness, taking liberties without invitation in the aggressive land seizures, characteristic of the overarching circumstances of colonization, casts the Shoyapee [Densmore] in the role of the unwanted ugly creature [the Frog Woman]." The player could see this explanation in a pop-up or collectible of some type and perhaps the player could, as Densmore, be cast in the role of the Frog Woman (as an avatar). If at any point the player catches a certain number of fish, then they must stop. Upon catching enough fish for Cogewea and her family, perhaps counted on a "responsibility meter," the player can gain experience points or another reward. The player might make choices in the game that change Densmore so that he doesn't have to be synonymous with the characteristics of colonization.[36] Perhaps the player can embody both Cogewea and Densmore in different parts of the game. Such is the power of a game world to offer both procedural and narrative options that can change the status quo of how Westerns are remediated into game worlds.

4 "He's Everything"

Making the Man in *L.A. Noire*

The title of this chapter pays homage to Lee Clark Mitchell's *Westerns*, in which he argues that the cowboy's body is the "delineation of masculinity."[1] Both Mitchell and Christine Bold agree that the Western is a defining genre of American masculinity, harnessing frontier ideals such as hardiness, progress, capitalism, stoicism, and white triumphalism to cisgender, straight, white male identity.[2] The cowboy in popular culture is most often represented as a "desirable object" to be both ogled and emulated.[3] Much like Owen Wister's greenhorn narrator who admires the Virginian's body, describing him as "a slim young giant, more beautiful than pictures," the player is invited to gaze at the virile body of *Red Dead Redemption*'s main player character John Marston by, for example, collecting outfits and, in turn, having him change into various forms of rugged masculinity, such as a gambler, bounty hunter, or gunslinger.[4] In the prequel (released in 2018), we play as Marston again, but this time, we can get a shave or a haircut, performing his masculinity more thoroughly. Print and film Westerns simply can't offer this kind of "embodied" scopophilia. That is, fans of print fiction and film (think *Star Wars*, *Star Trek*, and *Harry Potter* franchises) often engage in cosplay as a means to connect with and perform as beloved characters. Game worlds build this level of performativity into the story. Players can perform Marston's privileged white masculinity, which is, in real life, "the easiest difficulty level."[5] In contrast, *L.A. Noire* pits two cisgender, straight, white male descendants from the Western against each other in a type of grudge match. Cole Phelps is the straitlaced, intellectual police detective with a shady past, while Jack Kelso is the classic hard-boiled detective out to protect the little guy on the mean streets of the urban frontier.

Politics, Masculinity, and the Hard-Boiled Detective

This hegemonic model of masculinity not only dominates the Rockstar catalog but also the North American cultural field. While it is true that "culturally acceptable ways of being male are much broader," explains Elena Bertozzi, "[films], television shows, [video games], and advertisements portray men who are: hard, aggressive, competitive, violent, willing to sacrifice themselves for honor, desirous of rescuing females, unemotional, detached, etc."[6] Building on Bertozzi's work, I argue that this brute form of masculinity continues its popularity through the frontier logic of the hard-boiled or "tough thriller," a term coined by Frank Krutnik. The "tough thriller" form of noir tends to be concerned with the "lone male hero" who is at odds with the law and other social institutions, explains Krutnik. Krutnik contrasts the hero of the tough thriller with the police procedural detective, who is often set "in relation to systematized procedures."[7] This definition, in a nutshell, describes Kelso and Phelps.

L.A. Noire offers a game world that primarily remixes various elements from police procedurals and tough thrillers. Phelps is a combination of the police procedural and gentleman detective who depends on the rule of law, while Kelso is the hard-boiled private detective who is the "masculinisation of the classical detective."[8] By remixing but not countering the conventions of Hollywood noir, game worlds such as that of *L.A. Noire* performatively overvalue a form of American masculinity that is invariably anti-intellectual, misogynist, heteronormative, and violent. This cisgender, straight, white male hero is commonplace in gaming, explains Anastasia Salter and Bridget Blodgett, which is likely why the tough thriller is so appealing to game writers. *Max Payne*, for example, is a neo-noir franchise in which the eponymous player character's hegemonic masculinity is key to his revenge story. Salter and Blodgett's arguments about the ways in which the lone white male hero in game worlds is the "only character who gets to be embodied" is compelling, and my argument builds on their excellent work.[9] Male-centric literary genres, particularly those fueled by frontier mythology, control the way masculinity operates in game worlds like *Red Dead Redemption* and *L.A. Noire*. The type of masculinity that Salter and Blodgett discuss has a literary origin story.

John Pettegrew persuasively argues in *Brutes in Suits* that modern American aggressive masculinity is a "strategy for power taking" and not simply inherited aggressiveness. That is, the adage "boys will be boys" is false logic. For Pettegrew the evolutionary approach to gender where, for example, women are nurturing and men are aggressive is deeply flawed and ignores the role patriarchy, capitalism, and national discourses play in the construction of gender roles. He traces the "brutish turn in American character and masculinity" to Teddy Roosevelt's rough and rugged frontier masculinity. Roosevelt was in turn influenced by Frederick Jackson Turner's thesis "The Significance of the Frontier in American History" (1893), which frames American identity through the frontier myth.[10] Krutnik agrees, stating briefly that the world the hard-boiled detective "seeks to order is comparable to the mythologised 'Frontier' of the Western."[11] Pettegrew delves into the relationship between masculinity and the frontier myth in more detail than Krutnik, explaining that Turner's thesis influenced a certain way of understanding American masculinity and, more broadly, nationhood. More specifically, Turner's frontier thesis glorifies rugged masculinity, arguing for an ideal of masculine performance that has spread widely across the American cultural field. Rugged white straight masculinity is the default form of American masculinity, displacing heterogeneous forms at best and at worst defining other forms of masculinity as deviant. As a result, the political and social ideals harnessed to rugged masculinity, which can be described as decidedly individualistic and often neoliberal, are equally overvalued. These ideals are set in opposition to classic liberalism in *L.A. Noire*.

The ideals of classic liberalism most often expressed by Phelps are defined as effeminate, ineffectual, and even immoral. Classic liberalism seems to have fallen on hard times in twenty-first-century America, which is surprising considering the nation's founding ideals. America was conceived in liberalism and not liberty, where the autonomous individual can engage in freedom informed by rationality and equality.[12] This ideal, as defined under the law, adds Stephen Dilley, encourages American citizens to pursue life, liberty, and property.[13] This is not to say that liberalism is either emancipatory or egalitarian. To the contrary, American forms of liberalism tend to embrace capitalism, explains Lauren Berlant, which promises the good life but offers little in the way of social and economic means to live this so-called good life, such as buying property or even retiring, particularly for marginalized Americans.[14] bell hooks explains that classic liberalism makes assumptions that human nature is aggressive, dominating, and competitive, which not only valorizes stereotypical masculine traits but defines humanity as uncooperative, selfish, and individualistic.[15] In other words, liberalism is not a ticket to freedom or a "gateway" philosophy leading to lefty thinking. Quite the contrary, liberalism and neoliberalism are not that far apart in that both philosophies desire to secure individual rights and freedoms from state control.

The difference between the two philosophies rests in the conception of freedom. Where neoliberalism desires government to behave as a private enterprise that perceives everyday life through free-market philosophies (such as equating parenting, education, and healthcare with running a business); liberalism seeks to create citizens who can participate as rational, ethical social creatures who live largely free from interference from the state.[16] Educated, rational, and law abiding, Phelps is a liberal, whereas Kelso, much like Marston in *Red Dead Redemption*, understands that his liberty is contingent on market, corporate, and governmental forces (all intertwined) over which he has little to no power. Kelso knows that to eke out a small space of justice, he must sometimes break the law, which in turn reinforces his individualistic form of hard-boiled, tough-guy masculinity. This is a key element of the hard-boiled detective code, in which the hero is the "idealised and undivided figure of masculine potency and invulnerability."[17]

L.A. Noire has no love of liberalism. The game critiques liberalism through the failed masculinity embodied by its ostensible protagonist, Phelps. His masculinity is defined by his beliefs in a liberal conception of individualism, whereby he has inalienable rights that should give him the ability to live his life free from state corruption, inequality, and lawlessness. Following a model of enlightenment liberalism defined (most famously) by Jean Jacques Rousseau and John Locke and forming the foundation for U.S. conceptions of citizenship, Phelps assumes that state power is governed by rule of law.[18] These beliefs form the core of Phelps's self-conception as a police detective, which is shattered by the end of the game. Kelso, who the player learns is the actual hero and hard-boiled detective, sells a brand of neoliberal masculinity through gameplay that rejects Phelps's assumption of rationality, social contracts, and rule of law.

Nick Dyer-Witheford and Greig de Peuter discuss the role of neoliberalism in game worlds, with a focus on Rockstar's Grand Theft Auto: Vice City. While they note how the main character Tommy Vercetti embodies a brutish form of neoliberalism, they do not fully explain how his embodiment of rugged masculinity is furthered by what is essentially an urban frontier "characterized by the entrepreneurial city."[19] The gangster genre that the Grand Theft Auto franchise relies upon is based on true crime fiction and Hollywood noir elements. That is, Grand Theft Auto is a game world born out of genre conventions and certainly owes its take on masculinity, individualism, and free-market criminal activity to frontier ideologies. According to Pettegrew, Christine Bold, and to a lesser extent Krutnik, rugged individualism was harnessed to white masculinity through the frontier myth.

Neoliberalism protects economic interests over civil rights, civic duty, and equality and is therefore well aligned with the frontier myth, which sutures "nationhood to white male individualism" and capitalism. That is, the man on the make, who has ambition and drive trumps civic investment and engagement. Game stories fueled by the frontier myth rarely if ever offer players opportunities to better their worlds through civic duty or positively engage with political perspectives that seek to fetter capitalism;

instead, a lone hero saves individuals from encroaching state control and other nefarious individuals. I'm not suggesting that neoliberalism and the frontier myth engender one another, only that they pair well and are furthered and exemplified via a specific type of white masculinity. In "Neoliberal Masculinity," Gerald Voorhees agrees by defining hegemonic masculinity as "physical force and violence, occupational achievement, patriarchal domination of women and children, *the adventurous individualism of the frontiersman,* and heterosexuality."[20] This form of masculinity is envisioned as heroic, saving society from certain doom by evil and natural forces, and was popularized in the late eighteenth century in the form of the frontiersman figure.

Richard Slotkin has published extensive studies of the hard-boiled detective, a figure that he argues emerged from the frontier romances of the early national period and pulp Westerns of the late nineteenth and early twentieth centuries in the United States. In *Gunfighter Nation*, he argues that the hard-boiled detective story is "an abstraction of the essential elements of the Frontier Myth." He parallels the hard-boiled detective with the Virginian, both of which are "uncommon common men" who know "the world of crime as if from the inside but who also has a chivalric sense of honor."[21] In "The Sleuth and the Scholar," Slotkin parallels the hard-boiled detective with the frontiersman who helped to birth the Virginian, Marston, and Kelso: James Fenimore Cooper's wildly popular character Natty Bumppo, who appeared in Cooper's popular early nineteenth-century series of frontier romances. Cooper constructs Hawkeye as a liminal figure whose sense of honor is informed by his loyalty to his whiteness but who also understands "the Indian."[22] Kelso can easily be added to this list of frontier heroes who are liminal figures because he, like his predecessors, somewhat unwillingly protects the social order. The genre dictates that the hard-boiled detective can "move freely between these two worlds, without really being part of either," and Kelso does so frequently.[23] In fact, Slotkin's description of the hard-boiled detective's purpose dovetails with Kelso's moral code: "The hard-boiled detective's answer to the constriction and corruption of the post-Frontier landscape is to labor with wit and violence to create a small space or occasion in which something like traditional justice can prevail and in which the 'little man' or the 'good woman' can be protected against the malignity of the powers that be."[24]

While Kelso is able to uncover corruption and certainly protects the little guy "against the malignancy of the powers that be," he fails more than he achieves in terms of plot resolution—nothing much changes in his diegetic universe.[25] In fact, the final missions of game (when Kelso takes over as the main player character) make clear that where one corrupt corporate magnate is punished, there are more city officials and entrepreneurs to take his place. However, this failure does not affect Kelso's popularity as a potent figure of rugged masculinity.[26] The same cannot be said for Phelps; therefore, Kelso's function in the game narrative is not as much to save the day but more to exemplify what makes a man, which is what the hard-boiled detective is all about.[27]

Phelps, unlike Kelso, is deeply invested in upholding the law and protecting society from corruption. A good example of Phelps's desire to uphold the law, as any good police detective must, is in the cases located on the Vice Desk with dirty cop Roy Earle. Earle often has to warn Phelps to back off and stop threatening to arrest every criminal, advice Phelps finds confusing. Earle tries to explain the code of the street, a code Kelso knows well, but Phelps is only interested in legal systems. While Phelps's philosophy of law enforcement seems noble, his ideals are made to appear weak and even false as his ethos deteriorates: players have been documented as becoming increasingly dissatisfied with him as a player character over the course of the game.[28] The disappointment over Phelps's moral failings (for example, he cheats on his wife with the hapless heroin addict Elsa Lichtmann) is distressing to players because anthropomorphic agents such as player characters trigger the same parts of the brain that react to "everyday people to people interactions."[29] That is, to borrow Wayne Booth's terminology, player characters become friends we will defend. Why would Rockstar and the game development team from (the now-defunct) Team Bondi set the player up for disappointment in a main player character?

Because they are, wittingly or not, defining what makes the man, and in tough thrillers that's the hard-boiled detective, which Phelps is not. Players are thrust into a world that looks to be a classic Hollywood noir thriller with its "close and threatening urban settings"; as a result, players might be led to believe that their player character is equal to the challenge. But through flashbacks, players learn that Phelps is not the man he needs to be on the mean streets. These flashbacks define Phelps as an ambitious, intellectual, sanctimonious ass-kisser, the opposite of a hard-boiled detective. He is definitely not the urban embodiment of the frontier hero. In fact, *L.A. Noire* is unique in its juxtaposition of the intellectual liberal with the rugged masculinity of the hard-boiled detective. However, that comparison only becomes apparent late in the game.

At the beginning of the game, Phelps seems to fulfill both the gaming convention of the cisgender, straight, white male player character and the definition of rugged masculinity: he can recognize savagery, expose it, and rid its presence from the urban frontier. In other words, he can locate the "bad Indian" and eradicate this threat to the social order. Early in the game, Phelps's racial superiority and preternatural rationality is established through his encounter with Edgar Kalou, a murder suspect whose stereotypical performance of Jewish identity casts him as other. Through a peculiar type of goal-oriented gameplay, players learn to linguistically, culturally, and physically profile racialized others as actual or potential criminals.

The Win-Lose Conditions of White Masculinity

Phelps's cultural and social capital is physically, racially, and linguistically established in opposition to Kalou's exaggerated gestures, swarthy skin, and brash speech. Kalou is identified as Jewish, which is stereotypically foregrounded at every opportunity. He is the first character players interrogate, which establishes interrogation as a means for players to "read" identities through the white male gaze. When players perform as interrogators, they are expected to read facial expressions and in turn choose whether they doubt the suspect, believe them, or think they are lying. In the remastered game, the choices are even narrower: the player must choose between "good cop," "bad cop," and "accuse." In other words, players learn that as members of the police force (what Louis Althusser called the "repressive state apparatus"), they have the power to judge the speech acts of others as felicitous or not. Of course, players, in turn, are under the power of the script and code. If they choose to believe Kalou, they lose points; if they accuse him properly, they win rewards that make subsequent cases easier to solve. The rewards of the game are directly tied to the player's ability to position Kalou as an untrustworthy, irrational man.

Kalou's purpose is to do more than teach us about the procedures of interrogation as a game function; through gameplay, players are persuaded that Phelps is the better man. Where Kalou is a portrayed as a coward who runs away and surrenders with no resistance at all, Phelps chases his man and apprehends him at great personal risk.[30] Where Kalou smokes nervously and swears, Phelps is cool, calm, and clean. Because players are focalized through Phelps's perspective, they are aligned with his point of view, which categorizes Kalou under a deviant form of masculinity.

During the interrogation, Phelps implies that Kalou killed his nemesis Everett Gage for religious reasons. Kalou asserts that his Jewishness is his business in an apparently free country: "this isn't Germany," he yells. His response is hardly irrational; after all, the U.S. Constitution guarantees Kalou's right to religious freedom, but it is Kalou's performance of masculinity that pegs him as "un-American." For example, when Phelps implies he is communist, Kalou is furious, calling Phelps a "goy pud-snatcher." In fact, most of the Yiddish Kalou speaks is abusive, indicating to the player that not only is he irrational and hyperbolic, but his "ethnic" language is vulgar. He is, therefore, not a "good" man, even before he committed murder. Kalou makes it clear that he was harassed by Gage, through anti-Semitic slurs and shady business tactics, which gives us insight into the hierarchical order of race in the game. Phelps is somewhat sympathetic, but Kalou must pay. Phelps's sympathy plays into white liberal sentimentalism that acknowledges racism is wrong but also makes it clear that white power structures will solve the problem of racial strife. That is, Phelps—in these early cases—is the paragon of white liberal masculinity: rational, stoic, loyal, and strong, which is all verified through gameplay involving Kalou.

Through the initial (and lengthy) encounter with Kalou, players are actively persuaded through gameplay to connect ethnicity and race to deviant behavior. Further, because Phelps has not undergone the character assassination he suffers later in the game, the player forms an allegiance

7. COLE PHELPS AND MERLON OTTIE. *L.A. NOIRE.*

with Phelps. The term "allegiance" is usually used in film theory, but Petri Lankoski uses the term to note how players become morally and ethically aligned with a player character; in turn, the player becomes more accepting of the game's procedural rhetoric, which is deeply informed by the hard-boiled thriller.[31] In Raymond Chandler's and James Cain's tough thrillers, explains Megan Abbott, "the white male hero asserts his whiteness through distancing himself from perceived encroachment by, most especially, Mexican Americans, African Americans, and Asian Americans."[32] Through the interrogation mode of game play, players define race and race relations through the white male gaze.

While Kalou helps to define whiteness at the opening of the game, black male drug dealers further define racial hierarchies in a series of cases on the Vice Desk. Phelps and Earle interrogate one of the few black nonplayer characters with a speaking role, Merlon Ottie, who explains his role in a morphine racket: "The hebes took over the wire service and screwed me. Now I just do what I'm told—run numbers and shift dope. Jose is no different."

His role is clear: he works for Jewish mobsters in a subordinate role. A Latino man, Jose Ramez, supplies the hardware (radios and slot machines) the dope is transported in. The ranking of race in the game is black and Latino men at the bottom of the criminal marketplace, Jewish gangsters above them, and at the apex, white men, who are the only characters who can "be embodied as [people]."[33] Yet, while both Kelso and Phelps are both player characters, only one can claim to be a man's man.

Un-making the Man

While Phelps solves the morphine case (discussed more fully in chapter 6) through his powers of deduction and logic, these skills ultimately emasculate him. His triumphs are largely the result of his intellect, which isn't valued on the urban frontier. For example, Phelps catches a serial killer who is apparently the infamous Black Dahlia murderer by following a series of esoteric clues left by the killer. These clues can only be deciphered by correctly reading excerpts from Percy Bysshe Shelley's four-act lyrical play *Prometheus Unbound* (1820), which rewrites the Prometheus myth as a means to theorize how Romantic liberalism can deal with injustice. This metanarrative sheds light on Phelps's moral struggle in an unjust neoliberal frontier—he is a type of Prometheus figure, punished for defying the powers that be in that he refuses to let corruption go unpunished. Through Phelps's intellect and abilities of deduction (rivaled only by Sherlock Holmes), he solves the case. However, the serial killer is a member of the elite and is not prosecuted. This case and the subsequent cases involving police, corporate, and governmental corruption leave Phelps in a moral dilemma that he can't solve but that Kelso, as the hard-boiled detective, has no trouble deciphering.

By saying Kelso is *the* hard-boiled detective, I mean that his character matches the description of the hard-boiled figure given by Raymond Chandler, an author who contributed to developing this stock character:

Down these mean streets a man must go who is not himself mean, who is neither tarnished nor afraid. The detective in this story must be such a man. He's the hero. He's everything. He must be a complete man and a common man, yet an unusual man. He must be, to use a rather weathered phrase, a man of honor. He is neither a eunuch nor a satyr. I think he might seduce a duchess, and I'm quite sure he would not spoil a virgin. If he is a man of honor in one thing, he's that in all things. He is a relatively poor man, or he would not be a detective at all. He is a common man or he could not go among the common people. He has a sense of character or he would not know his job. He will take no man's money dishonestly and no man's insolence without due and dispassionate revenge. He is a lonely man, and his pride is that you will treat him as a proud man or be very sorry you ever saw him.[34]

Slotkin argues that much of this description could easily be applied to Cooper's frontiersman Hawkeye, and Kelso certainly follows his generic lead. Both can traverse between the "savage" or criminal worlds and back to civilization with ease; they are suspicious of women and domesticity but will protect women above all others; they are disdainful of authority and civilization but will defend civilization. Kelso is the seminal hard-boiled detective: "he's everything" in that he encompasses the aggressive, rugged masculinity overvalued in game worlds and, by extension, North American culture. Kelso stands in stark contrast to Phelps, who is progressively emasculated through a series of flashbacks and cutscenes.

Phelps's masculinity is undercut in two main ways: through gameplay and flashbacks, both of which further the central plotline about corruption and fraud. The first involves cutscenes accessed through collectible newspapers. Solving cases as Phelps, players find newspapers, which reveal parallel narrative action crucial to the central plotline. These newspapers act as portals that players enter, view a cutscene, and then exit back into the present time of the game. In the final missions, Phelps's narrative and the narrative action told via the newspaper converge. That is, while players solve cases as Phelps, the newspapers express parallel narrative action during the same time period. This kind of multi-linearity is common in game worlds, explains Marie-Laure-Ryan, that resist the linear and causal norms of narrative exposition.[35] Shira Chess argues that this resistance to narrative norms (such as a single climax and denouement to closure) in game worlds offers queer possibilities that can disrupt, for example, heteronormative values. While I agree that certain games offer queer possibilities by disrupting narrative norms, I remain skeptical that such disruption is possible game worlds like those of *L.A. Noire* and *Red Dead Redemption*. These game worlds incorporate genre conventions that triumph one type of masculinity and remix multiple genre conventions and narrative techniques to do so. In a sense, *L.A. Noire* remixes Hollywood noir in such a way that two stock characters: the hard-boiled detective and the police detective battle it out for straight white male primacy. This is certainly not a queering of male identities but entrenchment of the type of brute neoliberal masculinity Pettegrew defines.

The second set of narrative sequences are not revealed through collectibles gathered via gameplay but through flashbacks that occur at the start of most missions. The collectible newspapers and these flashbacks allow the player to enter two different narrative time sequences: one in the present time and one in the past. The flashbacks transport players back to World War II to witness Phelps's and Kelso's homosocial progression: Phelps fails to bond with his men, while Kelso excels at wartime bonding, enabling him to be an effective leader. Phelps shows himself to be inflexible and ignorant of what his men need, focusing solely on his own ambition and the army's bureaucratic requirements. In opposition, Kelso is keenly aware of situation and space, navigating his men through death-defying situations. There are many flashbacks and "newspaper stories," so I will limit the following discussion to a few key examples of how both the procedural rhetoric and narrative structure of this game world privileges one form of masculinity over another.

Pettegrew explains that war, particularly in the United States, has been a means to measure the value of a man in a homosocial environment; in other words, war is often represented as a man-making activity rather than a traumatic, destructive force.[36] War also yokes masculinity to patriotism, strength, violence, and courage: a good soldier is a good American man who doesn't desire advancement but what's best for his country and brothers in arms. Dennis Broe argues that Hollywood noir tended to express the patriotic bonding of brothers to protect democracy and also challenged the "syrupy portrayal" of such films by exposing the class and gender contradictions that wartime tended to exacerbate.[37] *L.A. Noire* plays both sides of the noir coin. Phelps is the over-privileged, college-educated officer, and Kelso is the ahistorical individualistic hero who saves his men from Phelps's ineptitude.

The first two flashbacks create tension between the player's allegiance to Phelps as a classic detective and his clear ambitions in the army. In the first flashback, players learn that Phelps wants to be an officer, while Kelso just wants to serve his country alongside his fellow brothers in arms. These flashbacks reveal Phelps's shameful past, where he kowtows to his superiors at the expense of his fellow soldiers. Phelps tells Kelso that he doesn't have what it takes to be an officer and Kelso heartily agrees. He leaves officer training and tells Phelps he is joining a rifle company to "fight the real war." Kelso joins the enlisted men, creating the type of homosocial bond at which Phelps fails miserably. Phelps has fundamentally misunderstood what makes a man. It's not intellectualism and ambition but consistent self-presentation as a hard-boiled figure of "masculine potency and invulnerability."[38]

In yet another flashback, players discover the level of Phelps's privilege and distance from the ideal of rugged masculinity. As he is shipping out, Phelps shares with Hank, his fellow officer, that while his family owns a shipping business, Phelps has never been on a ship. He then compares himself to Odysseus, venturing out "into the American century" to rule the world. Hank corrects Phelps's misinterpretation of what makes a man in wartime: they need to "remember their jobs," which is to survive and keep their men alive. This flashback defines Phelps's education and intellectualism as misguided; the story of Odysseus is self-aggrandizing and won't save lives. Phelps is therefore pegged as one of the elite who doesn't care about the "little guy." This exchange is proven true by flashbacks shown later in the game story in which Kelso saves Phelps's life, affirming Kelso's authority as the hero.

If the initial set of flashbacks defines Phelps as an ambitious over-educated twit, then the final set of flashbacks ensures we know he is a terrible leader and therefore a failure as a man. In the present time of the game, the above flashback occurs just before the player leaves Phelps as the player character and Kelso becomes the embodied character. Therefore, this flashback operates as a means to provide the final justification for the player's rejection of Phelps as the liberal intellectual and their ultimate allegiance to Kelso. Similarly, the newspaper plotlines that involve Kelso exemplify his superior masculinity, encouraging players to ally with Kelso and disengage from Phelps.

As a brief aside, the newspaper as the medium through which the player gains access to the major plotline of the story provides an interesting metaphor for the convergence between old and new media. When the player uses the controller to pick up the newspaper, they become participants in the furthering of the story. In a sense, the game exemplifies Henry Jenkins's theory of convergence culture that we are no longer passive media consumers but active media producers traversing overlapping and multilayered media landscapes.[39] Merging three media forms (print, film, and the video game) in the representation of a newspaper, the game enacts convergence culture, making players feel like active participants, and they are, but only in a limited sense. Robert Farrow explains that while total immersion is simply a techno-fantasy, the controller does facilitate interaction with objects in the game through players' physical actions.[40] Players must perform the act of directing Phelps to retrieve the newspaper and hold it up. In order to achieve the coveted 100 percent game completion, players must gather all the newspapers. These actions encourage players to pay attention to the cutscenes the newspapers reveal. The newspapers as collectibles are an integral part of the procedural rhetoric of the game, persuading players to value Kelso over Phelps and thereby valorizing the hard-boiled detective over the police detective.

I want to focus on only one of the newspaper narratives, in which players learn that Courtney Sheldon, a medic who served under Phelps and Kelso in the war, partners with the infamous mobsters Mickey Cohen and Johnny Stompanato. Sheldon has been selling stolen army-issue morphine to the mobsters in order to give money to his fellow veterans and also pay for medical school, an ambition that causes Cohen to quip, "You wanna be a doctor and a drug peddler; interesting combination, huh?" However, Sheldon wants to sever ties with Cohen and take the dope off the streets, which causes Cohen to put a hit out on Sheldon. He then turns to Kelso (not Phelps) for help.[41]

Kelso reveals his expert understanding of the criminal world by explaining to Sheldon that "the only thing these guys understand is force, Sheldon. They got to the top back East by proving to be more vicious than the English, the Irish, and the Dutch. They make their own laws. That's the nature of a secret society." Kelso is a claims investigator for California Fire and Life—how would he know so much about the mob? But this preternatural knowledge is part and parcel of his frontiersman lineage. Like Hawkeye, he simply knows how to deal with "savages." Like the Virginian, he is the natural aristocrat who simply knows how to use registers of language and violence expertly. Like Sam Spade, he simply knows how the underworld works and can master any situation.[42]

In the next scene, Sheldon and Kelso meet with Cohen in a dark alleyway. These cutscenes start out in black and white, the classic color scheme of film noir, capturing the shadow and darkness of a corrupt urban environment. However, these scenes gradually turn to a "realistic" color saturation, giving them a higher truth value or modality. That is, the noir environment in which Kelso can thrive is not in the historical modality of black and white but the realistic color scheme of the present. In this scene, players learn that Kelso is not only fearless but also erudite. Unlike Phelps, Kelso's intelligence does not render him an outsider. When Kelso meets up with the gangsters to negotiate Sheldon's release from their agreement, he quotes the duke of Wellington at the Battle of Waterloo. Clearly, the ability to decipher Shelley's poetry to solve the murders of six women is not as manly as quoting a general from a historical battlefield. The intellectual lines have been drawn: Kelso's form of intellectualism is far more masculine than Phelps's apparently effeminate ability to cite and analyze verse.

Kelso successfully deals with the mobsters through his linguistic prowess and expert use of force. As Kelso walks away, Cohen tries to emasculate Kelso, to which Sheldon explains to Cohen, and to the player, that Kelso "killed six Japs hand-to-hand with just a bayonet and a KA-BAR knife. His outfit, the Sixth Marines, killed over 100,000 Japs in 3 months in Okinawa and he was in the thick of it." Cohen responds, "Those Japs are those little guys," to which Sheldon retorts, "Yes, Mr. Cohen, about your size." The implications are clear: all enemies are comparable on the urban frontier. Japanese soldiers and Jewish mobsters are an evil that can be wiped out easily by the hard-boiled detective but not by the rule-bound police detective.

When Kelso and Phelps finally meet up, Kelso tries to get Phelps to stop feeling guilty for his poor leadership in the war (which led to several soldiers' deaths): "Courage isn't a tap you can turn on or off. Courage isn't permanent. It's a tenuous and fickle thing. Courage and cowardice exist in every man.

Get over it." While Kelso's words may sound reasonable, they really are not. Kelso is the very definition of what Voorhees calls neoliberal masculinity and Pettegrew and Bertozzi describe as brute masculinity: a man protects the urban frontier; he does his duty; he is strong and can fight; he is stoic. In other words, a man "gets over it."

After tutelage from Kelso and learning that rugged masculinity is the only way to combat corruption in the neoliberal world, Phelps now plays the role of the hard-boiled detective. Sheldon has been murdered, and as Earle approaches the body, Phelps confronts Earle, telling him to stay away from the body or he'll "blow [his] fucking head off." This is the first time we've heard Phelps swear, signifying his transformation into brute masculinity. As Phelps performs his neoliberal masculinity correctly, he is once again allowed to take over as the player character, sharing the gameplay stage with Kelso. Phelps may sacrifice himself at the end of the game, but the message is clear: rugged, hard-boiled masculinity can and should be learned. This is a chilling lesson indeed, particularly considering the toxicity of gamer culture, in which such forms of brute masculinity are heralded.

5 Blanching Noire

The Performance of White Womanhood and Middle-Class Identity

In the previous chapter, I argued that the hard-boiled detective figure, powered by his frontiersman ancestry, not only polices gender norms (pardon the pun) but also shuts down intellectualism, queerness, and liberalism. In this chapter, a particular set of cases on the homicide desk offers an opportunity to discuss how a durable literary genre like Hollywood noir defines gender roles through gameplay.[1] These cases could very well be classified as a specific subgenre of Hollywood noir called "social problem" films, in which social issues such as alcoholism, racism, and mental illness are "contained."[2] The social issue on the homicide desk that needs to be "contained," a rather chilling word in this context, is the transgressive behavior of predominantly white women. The main player character, Detective Cole Phelps—promoted from the traffic desk to homicide—discovers that each victim, in life and death, has threatened the status of her middle-class family. Noir fiction and film commonly "[patrols] the boundaries of gender and mobility" through the detective figure, and *L.A. Noire* follows suit, structuring gameplay to follow genre conventions.[3] Through hunting for clues (while straddling naked, mutilated, and murdered women) and interrogating witnesses and suspects, the procedural rhetoric of this game world argues on the side of an old patriarchal chestnut that women are "asking for it."

It might be tempting to dismiss the treatment of women in the game as part and parcel of the time period, but such arguments are fallacious. Fictional narratives are not required to pledge fealty to the inequalities of the time periods they dramatize. However, if this kind of logic is bothersome, then consider that there were noir fiction and film where women were more than femme fatales or damsels in distress, sometimes even taking up the mantle of the hard-boiled detective. I wonder what gameplay might have looked like had head writer Brendan McNamara decided to include elements from Cornell Woolwich's novels *Black Angel* (1940) or *The Phantom Lady* (1942), both of which were made into films and feature strong female detective figures.[4] But no, *L.A. Noire*'s gameplay is decidedly patriarchal and even misogynist.

It's Elementary

On the homicide desk, Phelps's powers of deduction bear a striking resemblance to those of the classical detective figure, meaning he dispels "magic and mystery" through apparent scientific method and logical deduction, both of which are the stereotypical domain of white men.[5] As noted in chapter 4, Phelps is not the classic hard-boiled detective figure in this noir thriller but the classic police detective from the noir style of police procedural. On the homicide desk, Phelps seems to be both the preternaturally rational classical detective and the rule-bound, objective police detective. While it's true that the police procedural detective depends on science and logic, Phelps uses powers of deduction and interpretation more akin to Sherlock Holmes than the more gritty documentary style of systematic police work found in the 1940s police procedural.[6]

The detective figure's claim to rationality, argues Catherine Belsey, is often not supported by anything other than an exclamation of "Elementary!" or "I've got it!" rendering the detective less a figure of actual logic and more

8. INTERROGATION. *L.A. NOIRE.*

a means to entrench archaic patriarchal values (e.g., men are rational and women are not).[7] As the voice of reason and rationality, Phelps narrates these dead women's lives, turning their existence into easily digestible case notes. Through Phelps, players learn that these women destroyed themselves and, by extension, their families through their lack of self-control. These women violated the sanctity of their middle-class lives by corrupting their domestic purity.

Does Gender Matter in Video Games?

Perhaps gender doesn't matter in all games, but when a game remediates and remixes the modern Western and noir genres, then gender matters a great deal. Carolyn Miller and Amy Devitt have both argued that genres tell the audience what to expect in rhetorical and social situations. Frank Krutnik and Dennis Broe have made it clear that American forms of noir work to define gender and class within strict, normative parameters. When genres are made playable, their cultural work is amplified. For example, players are rewarded with intuition points when they perform the role of the cisgender, straight, white male detective correctly, assessing whether suspects and witnesses are lying or not.

These intuition points enable players to find clues with more ease and in turn gain more points. Rewards are persuasive. Because the player must perform as the detective figure, the player not only is dropped into the ideological framework of the noir narrative but also receives rewards for performing optimally within the gendered conventions of the genre.

While print texts and film can only desire to represent, computer software can "represent process with process."[8] Therefore, game systems do not inscribe gender but replicate the constitution of gender through "the stylization of the body" and "the mundane way in which bodily gestures, movements, and enactments of various kinds constitute the illusion of an abiding gendered self."[9] Put another way, games replicate the conventional bodily movements and gestures of gender, such as the swinging hips of a woman wearing high heels. Can players really be so immersed in a game that their perspective and perhaps even performance of gender are influenced?

Robert Farrow is skeptical, explaining that even though players may embody Cole Phelps, they are not simulating an experience but playing as part of a fictional story. That is, players do not actually believe they "embody" Phelps; however, they do perform as Phelps by engaging in goal-oriented actions, reacting to and interacting with other characters to progress through missions or perhaps lose points and therefore rewards such as intuition points or a new suit that offers more abilities.[10] Whether or not players "embody" Phelps (or the other protagonist, Jack Kelso) is not the issue. What is at issue is how the game persuades the player that gender performance in this game world is not only plausible but persuasive. Like the majority of game worlds, *L.A. Noire* only gives players the option to control cisgender, straight, white male characters; however, female non-player characters break from gaming conventions on the homicide desk. In many game worlds, NPCs are most commonly part of escort missions, where the white male player character must get these damsels in distress safely from point A to point B.[11] On the homicide desk, the damsels in distress have been raped, mutilated, or murdered. They were attacked when alone, often drunk, and as a result seemingly deserve their fates. This form of representation is particularly disturbing considering that when men play games that objectify women, they tend to believe rape myths such as that the victim deserved the crime.[12]

Victoria Beck and colleagues peg the realism in a game world as a major influence on players' belief systems, but genre is also culpable.[13] Game worlds most often make the player character a white male of exceptional abilities: this convention is a controlling feature of gaming and is doubly true for game worlds based on male-centric literary genres, such as Westerns and noir film and fiction. While video games have begun to include more single-player female heroes, such as Guerilla Games' *Horizon Zero Dawn* (2017) and EA's *Battlefront 2* (2018), these examples are few and far between. The problem is getting worse, though, with only 5 percent of all video games featuring a female protagonist in 2019.[14] On *L.A. Noire*'s homicide desk, female NPCs are not simply murdered damsels in distress.

The murder victims Phelps investigate take on the generic traits of the femme fatale archetype. They asserted their independence and had desires beyond being wives and mothers, and a couple had careers. In the postwar period, explains Ken Hillis, Hollywood noir was a historical movement that helped make sense of the world through its formula of order, chaos, and a return to order; more importantly, many noir films, particularly the hard-boiled variety, provided the audience with a sympathetic protagonist who suffered existential angst over his inability to access the American Dream. The hard-boiled detective enabled postwar audiences to feel superior in their ability, for the most part, to access this dream, comprising progress and success, which was evidenced by homeownership, marriage, and accumulation. The femme fatale is an obstacle to this access, and for her refusal to play her part as submissive wife and mother, she is punished, which in turn aligns the audience with the patriarchal norms.[15]

Joan Copjec explains that Hollywood noir quelled "paranoia regarding the [postwar] working woman's place in society."[16] It's not a stretch to suggest that Hollywood noir punishes women for daring to be strong and independent, portraying such independence through the figure of the femme fatale as a challenge to masculine identity and stereotypical ideals of femininity and domesticity. After all, she attempts to ruin "the lives of men and is at the same time the victim of her own lust for enjoyment."[17] Elizabeth Cowie argues that Hollywood noir film and fiction operate as a psychical coping mechanism in response to the rise in female power postwar.[18] Taking up this cause, *L.A. Noire* allays fears of feminism and by extension diversity in game worlds, killing off apparent threats to white male privilege.

The femme fatale NPCs on the homicide desk were murdered for daring to be active agents in their own lives. That is, they refused to be rendered passive objects of desire by the male gaze.[19] To add insult to injury, this "active agency" is defined as immoral or at least reckless. These women were heavy drinkers, schemers, shopaholics, and alcoholics. They are often portrayed as making poor decisions by wearing suggestive clothing or leaving a bar or a party unescorted. Akin to blaming rape victims for what they wear or how they behave, the game storyline frames these women as partly responsible for their own murders. Had they simply done what they were told, they would not be mutilated, raped, and murdered. I found playing this narrative sequence disturbing and difficult, not only because I had to straddle mutilated women and investigate their bodies, but also because the game urged me to blame these women for making poor choices and destroying their families.

If the initial historical reason for the creation of the femme fatale was to quash paranoia over female economic and social independence, then *L.A. Noire*'s plethora of femme fatales would seem to respond to the post-collapse rise in the number of U.S. women who are the family breadwinners.[20] Anastasia Salter and Bridget Blodgett describe the ways many game worlds define anything associated with femininity as weakness or integrate women as nothing more than hypersexualized props. *L.A. Noire*'s homicide desk follows this paradigm but from within the parameters of Hollywood noir. As I stated earlier, a plethora of games feature the cisgender, straight, white male as the key savior for white women.[21] Phelps fits this bill, except he is a detective, so he doesn't save but instead rationally explains why white women (and one Latina) have been raped, mutilated, and murdered. Time and again, Phelps learns that these women engaged in "loose" behavior, which put them in the path of a serial killer.

This game fuses the figure of the femme fatale with the expectations of classic American domesticity. While the femme fatale is often a vocal, central figure with a strong voice in Hollywood noir, she is nothing more than a corpse graced with the occasional flashback on the homicide desk. Victims' lives are most often narrated via their husbands, the coroner, Phelps, or his misogynist partner, Rusty Galloway. As the game progresses, players discover that each woman has destroyed her family unit, which certainly fits the bill of the femme fatale figure in Hollywood noir; however, they were also wives and mothers, meaning they were expected to conform to the standards of what Lauren Berlant calls "women's culture" in the United States. Berlant explains that women's culture is an intimate public sphere that operates much like "white paternalism, sometimes dressed as maternalism."[22] This intimate sphere is crucial to the functioning of conventional American white middle-class values, including conformity, safety, sentimentality, and accumulation. By representing this sphere on the homicide desk as broken and corrupt, the game continues a long-standing literary and cultural tradition of using white women as metonymic substitutions for the nation, who often appear as part of a signifying chain of meaning that defines womanhood as inextricably connected with the American home and domesticity.

Each murder case on the homicide desk starts in classic noir style with "unusual angles" and chiaroscuro, creating a decentered and unstable composition.[23] Each case also begins with a woman being murdered using these classic visual elements; for example, in the first case, murder victim Celine Henry is dragged from a car and then bludgeoned to death with a tire iron. Players only see the killer's feet and then the shadowy outline of him beating her to death. This cutscene voyeuristically frames female characters as passive objects of desire and male characters as active agents.[24] While Laura Mulvey's work in how the male gaze operates in Hollywood cinema has undergone a great deal of criticism for its strict dichotomy between male acts of looking and female objectification, *L.A. Noire* engages in exactly the kind of classic scopophilic cinematic apparatus she critiques, as shown when players follow the camera eye to the debriefing room at the station, where Captain Donnelly fills Phelps in on the Celine Henry case.

The scene changes from classic black-and-white noir camera angles when Celine is murdered to full color; from odd camera angles to a straight shot of the room where Phelps and his fellow detectives receive their cases. Players transition from voyeuristically watching a murder to gameplay, or put another way, from helplessly watching chaos to performing as the active agent that quells chaos, the detective. As Phelps, players of any gender and sexuality have the power to investigate and demand answers to questions; they have access to knowledge, but that knowledge is parceled out by the game mechanics, such as through interrogations. Players are confined by the procedural rhetoric of the game to accept whatever win-lose conditions they must engage with to move the story forward. The game constants are controlled by the genre elements, which have a national history and origin.

I mentioned at the start of this chapter that the homicide desk in *L.A. Noire* revives the "social problem" noir thriller. However, the type of social problem these cases expose and try to contain has a long narrative history in the United States. *L.A. Noire* exhumes nineteenth and early twentieth-century debates over temperance and sobriety. Discourses of alcoholism in U.S. popular culture define "norms of proper and 'healthy' masculinity and femininity." Only one of the victims is a labeled alcoholic, but the majority are heavy drinkers or certainly had been drinking the night they were murdered. The formulaic narrative of the alcoholic marriage, a common trope in mid-twentieth-century film and literature, changed the American temperance narrative from external forces causing mayhem in the American home to internal marital drama.[25] *L.A. Noire* shifts the victim of intemperance from the long-suffering wife of an alcoholic husband to the long-suffering husband of an alcoholic wife.

Temperance literature often portrayed drunkards' wives as sympathetic if not pathetic, but by the postwar period, with the medicalization of alcoholism and advent of social work, doctors began focusing on marriage as the site of therapy rather than solely on the alcoholic partner, and as a result the trope of the alcoholic marriage was born.[26] Fast-forward to the twenty-first century, and *L.A. Noire* makes this trope of the alcoholic marriage part of gameplay. If players interrogate hapless, grieving husbands and witnesses correctly, then players learn that these women ignored the pleas of their families in favor of going out for a few drinks. As these cases unfold, these women are shown to be partly to blame for their violent deaths through their reckless behavior.

Victims are often and disturbingly compared to Elizabeth Short, more commonly known as the Black Dahlia. Her heretofore unsolved case is solved in this game world. This "what if" scenario makes the other murders seem even more realistic, and in sum, all of the murders together operate as a warning about female sexuality and power. Through the iconic figure of the Black Dahlia, the game supplies historical credibility to the ideology that women are a danger to themselves and others unless they are kept under control: their sexuality apparently brings forth bestial behavior in men. Linking these murdered intemperate women to the Dahlia murder is more than simply sensationalism: Elizabeth Short was characterized in the media as a starlet who drank and caroused. In 1947 (the year the game world is set in), her dismembered, bled, and mutilated body was found in Leimert Park, Los Angeles, and caused a media sensation. The press's name for her, "Black Dahlia," not only gave her an air of mystery and eroticism but also metaphorically characterized her sexuality as dangerous, particularly when considering the metaphorical connections conventionally made between vulvas and flowers. She was cast in "a wider narrative of Hollywood in the 1940s: one in which beautiful young women with big aspirations met tragic ends." Photographs of Short also position her as a real-life dark and beautiful femme fatale, rendering her as a real-life example of a woman whose lack of self-control led to her grisly death.[27] In other words, Short's appearance in the game creates an "interface between a person [or player] and a historical narrative."[28]

This suturing of an individual into a larger history usually happens in a museum or a movie theater, explains Alison Landsberg, but this affective suturing is also the domain of many game worlds, transporting a player into an apparently historically accurate narrative.[29] Landsberg calls this process of affective attachment within public cultural memory "prosthetic memory": the memory may not be of our experience, but we will incorporate it into our psyche and use this psychical prosthesis to construct our identities. Most certainly, Short's story is a pervasive form of public cultural memory.

"Prosthetic memory" is also the term that defines the mass mediation of memory. Holocaust museums and other forms of careful and ethically mediated mass remembrance of traumatic events are a far different matter from the kind of historical play encountered on the homicide desk. The myth of the Black Dahlia is a collective means to contain and regulate female sexuality into clear parameters: white women who are sexually active, drink alcohol, and hang out at bars will pay the price. White women who don't are safe and secure in the national home.

Weak Sisters, Bad Dames

How does this misogynistic paradigm play out in the game? As Phelps heads out to investigate Celine's body, Galloway mentions the Black Dahlia case. Galloway surmises that the Henry case has nothing to do with the Dahlia murders, explaining that "90 percent of murders are domestic." Phelps asks why so many women are being murdered this year to which Galloway responds, "'Cause of the war. You should know that. Guy gets to kill people every day in combat, comes home, and he's expected to take lip from his wife? What do you think is going to happen?" Galloway's comments fit into the "men can't help it" or evolutionary excuse for domestic violence and rape: this exchange is an example of biological determinism, which excuses responsibility for domestic violence and rape culture. If a woman "gives lip" to a traumatized man, then she can expect to be beaten or perhaps even murdered; after all, "boys will be boys."

When Phelps approaches the crime scene, players see a brief aerial shot of the victim, who is naked and mutilated. As required by the game mechanics, Phelps straddles Celine Henry in order to check her body for clues. This pattern of investigation is a convention of the game, but to straddle a naked, mutilated woman's body enters a new realm of voyeurism and scopophilia.

As Phelps straddles the body, we hover over his shoulder, observing his manipulation of Celine Henry's face, hands, and torso. On a personal note, I found this part of the game difficult to play, not only because of the gruesome condition of the bodies, but because of the bareness of the dichotomy

9. COLE PHELPS STRADDLING A BODY. *L.A. NOIRE.*

between female passivity and male action. The killer has carved the initials "BD" into Henry's torso, and when the coroner suggests the initials might stand for the Black Dahlia, Henry is then sutured to the Black Dahlia narrative. Henry, too, was a "loose woman" with aspirations she couldn't fulfill, which in turn means that Henry was, at least in part, accountable for her rape, mutilation, and murder.

At each crime scene involving a heavy drinker, players find a clue leading to the bar she frequents, and soon Phelps is on his way to Henry's favorite bar, The Bamba. The bartender tells Phelps that Henry frequented the club most nights, and with this statement her character is established. Phelps then interrogates the club owner Dick McColl, who paints a picture of Henry as a "lovely woman" but also as a heavy drinker who had "quite a head start" before she met up with a man at the bar. He mentions Henry's husband, who then become a person of interest, a label that pops up at the bottom of the screen.

The text at the bottom right of the screen operates as an internal narrator, providing clues, locations, and possible suspects, directing players to frame characters as innocent or guilty. As soon as the algorithm is activated, a character becomes categorized as a suspect, but what leads a character to become a suspect is often based on genre convention. Hollywood noir in the late forties often depicted the destruction of families and middle-class bliss.[30] Later, players discover that the serial killer frames husbands for their wives' murders. Galloway condemns these men as "weak sisters" for not controlling their wives. More importantly, as Phelps tracks Henry's whereabouts on the night of her murder, Phelps assassinates her character through the clues found via gameplay. Of course, this is a rhetorical choice on the part of the game narrative and mechanics. What would the game have been like if it didn't continuously suggest that these women had a hand in their own murders?

For example, to make headway in the game, players need to ask questions about Henry's behavior and background, which uncovers her heavy drinking and infidelity. But here's another angle: players also know she was a pilot—what if they could learn more about her life as an aviator rather than a barfly? Only certain aspects of Henry's life deserve attention, such as when Phelps discovers during his investigation of the body that Henry is missing a ring, usually a symbol of passionate attachment. Subsequently, Phelps interrogates the bar owner, McColl, about the ring, which he describes as "on the large side, larger than life, like Celine herself." Interrogation scenes have win-lose conditions, which means players, as the detective, must assess McColl's truthfulness by choosing "truth," "doubt," or "lie." The procedural rhetoric of the game rhetorically positions Phelps as the authoritative subject as per genre requirements and McColl—as yet another cisgender, straight, white male—as a reliable resource. Players discover that McColl bought Henry the ring, revealing her adultery. Phelps's credibility increases as Henry's decreases, even though she is the rape and murder victim.

Celine's ethos drops further after Phelps investigates the house and questions the neighbors. Players learn that Henry was very drunk by 10:00 p.m. and her husband, Jacob Henry, may have given her a black eye. Galloway comments that Jacob did the right thing hitting his wife, stating that if his wife drank that much, he'd give her a smack. Phelps doesn't buy into Galloway's rhetoric. However, the neighbor defends Jacob, who takes up the position of the suffering spouse in the alcoholic marriage, a role, as a mentioned earlier, usually reserved for wives. The neighbor calls Jacob "long-suffering" and tells Phelps that Celine drove very drunk, a cardinal sin, lowering Celine's ethos even more.

Phelps arrests Jacob, who insists he wanted to send Celine for treatment because he knew he could not handle her drinking problem on his own. Jacob's innocence is confirmed when players learn that Celine was not killed by blunt force trauma to the head, which was the suspected cause of death; instead, her death was sexually violent and gruesome. Malcolm Carruthers, the coroner, tells Phelps that "death was from hemorrhage; the shock from the fractured ribs and multiple injuries caused by stomping.... [The killer's] some kind of sex fiend. The tissues of the anus were bruised about an eighth, but no trace of semen in the anus, vagina, or stomach." This scientific explanation of homicide by a coroner is a classic element of the police procedural. This game world remixes noir elements because game worlds have a unique ability to layer multiple plotlines in ways that experimental print and film can only dream of. Novels can layer multiple plotlines to an extent, but novels don't have teams of developers to create robust, multilayered fictional universes like those of *L.A. Noire* or *Red Dead Redemption*. An apt analogy might be to imagine a television series like *Breaking Bad* and its spin-off *Better Call Saul* (maybe throwing in elements of *The Wire* for good measure) remixed into one fictional world that a player can enter and interact within. Multiple forms of Hollywood noir are remixed in *L.A. Noire*. Therefore, the coroner of the police procedural can interact with the classic detective figure on the homicide desk. In other desks in the game, such as vice and arson, various forms of noir are remixed. However, I digress.

Celine's punishment for her "wild" behavior is rape and murder. The real killer, Garrett Mason, frames Jacob. Despite mounting evidence that Jacob is innocent, Captain Donnelly does not care; as far as he is concerned, Jacob was a browbeaten husband, which means he was pushed to murder his wife. In the United States, marriage has specific and distinctive national roles, and "it is the vehicle through which the apparatus of the state can shape the gender order." In *L.A. Noire* the man is supposed to be the head of the household, and the woman acquiesces to the man, but these victims do not follow that order. Captain James Donnelly calls the victims' husbands "sob sisters." Donnelly has the authority to dictate the narrative of this marriage because marriage is not private but public, "underlying national belonging and the cohesion of the whole." The United States has a historical commitment to "exclusive and faithful monogamy, preferably intraracial," which in turn creates a unifying moral standard.[31]

Further, this insistence on the purity of the marriage contract extends to the political ordering of household and by extension the nation. The heated debates over gay marriage in the United States speak to the common perception that a man's responsibility as the head of the house "qualified him to be a participating member of the state," which in turn has led to the "insistence on traditional marriage as a necessary pillar of the nation."[32] However, Jacob queers the heteronormative marriage contract by acting as the caregiver to his alcoholic wife: he is not meant to be the civilizer but the protector of civilization. Jacob has failed as a husband. His failure invites Phelps to echo Donnelly's and Galloway's insults and categorize Jacob as a failed man by calling him a "weak sister" during interrogation gameplay. Phelps accuses Jacob of murdering his wife and does so despite knowing that Jacob is innocent. If Phelps frees Jacob and bucks the system, players won't gain intuition points. Again, a game's procedures are set up to encourage the player to collect achievements and progress through the game, but players only win rewards by ideologically positioning themselves correctly within genre expectations.

While the focus is on Jacob, lingering in the background is Celine's drinking, personal ambition, and possible adultery, meaning that she is, at least in part, responsible for her murder and the destruction of her family. Jacob admits to "killing her dreams" to be a pilot, but in exchange, he offers "security" to Celine. In the post-9/11 and post–economic collapse era, the idea of security has multiple meanings, playing on ideas of financial and national security, both of which are precarious at best. Noir deals well with such instabilities; as Dennis Broe explains it, Hollywood noir expressed

10. THERESA TARALDSEN BEING STALKED. *L.A. NOIRE.*

middle-class resistance to the faceless moral authority of corporations and state apparatuses, and this version of Hollywood noir has its fingerprints all over *L.A. Noire.*[33] "Security" implies conformity to rules and standards; therefore, when Jacob describes his upward mobility from his humble origins as a tenant farmer to his current middle-class status, his social mobility and hard work renders Celine's aviation dreams as wasteful, extravagant, and intemperate.

This pattern of investigation continues for the next three cases: transgressive women are raped and murdered, homes are broken, children left motherless, and husbands are shamed. For example, Theresa Taraldsen (like Celine Henry) is a "good time girl," whom Lars Taraldsen married because she "was so much fun but now she drives [him] fucking crazy."

Marriage is not about "good times" but responsibility and conventional behavior. Theresa became noncompliant within the conventions of women's culture, and the result is not simply her diminishment through, for example, shaming, but her death. Her shaming occurs posthumously, and like those of all the other victims, her story serves as a parable to all cisgender, straight, white women.

While Celine's case sets the pattern of investigation of intemperate wives and mothers, three other cases diverge enough from this pattern of murdered-femme-fatale-blames-husband-exposes-moral-failures to warrant further discussion. These cases further neoliberal claims that socialism "promised a false and morally repellent freedom from economic necessity at the cost of limited life choices and an inevitable descent into totalitarianism."[34] Players run into socialist-leaning (white) male characters on the homicide desk, who are represented as predatory and amoral. When players investigate the Evelyn Summers murder, they run into Grosvenor McCaffrey, an intellectual whose education has tainted his worldview. In fact, both Grosvenor and Evelyn are failures: the former is an intellectual socialist, while the latter is alcoholic, homeless, and, worst of all, a forty-year-old unwed woman.

Evelyn's failure as a white middle-class woman is reinforced by a letter from her mother that Phelps finds at the crime scene. Players can read it or not, but it is entered into the case notes, and as such it is a clue worth possible rewards:

Dear Evelyn,
I hope this letter finds you in a better way than when we last parted. Bitter words were exchanged. You had taken too much liquor and we both know what that makes you become. But I am not writing to harass and accuse. I am writing to apologize. I was heartbroken seeing what had become of my little girl, what she is doing to herself. You are destroying your body and your soul with liquor, Evelyn, and it is harder for me to watch than you can imagine.

Evelyn's mother offers her a second chance to follow her mother's legacy as a good wife and mother, but instead, Evelyn wanted a career, a fact reinforced by memorabilia from her working life, such as her desk title plaque. The inclusion of her mother's letter in the game is a prime example of what Henry Jenkins calls "convergence culture," where old and new media collide.[35]

A letter is an intimate object, usually meant for one person's eyes. As the detective figure, players are given access into the intimate sphere of victim's lives. Voyeuristically, players come to understand Evelyn's social

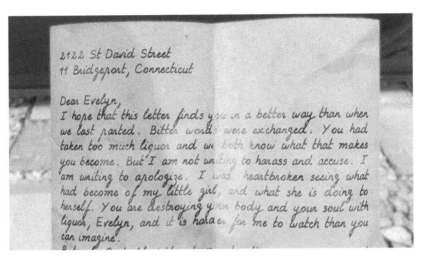

2122 St David Street
11 Bridgeport, Connecticut

Dear Evelyn,
I hope that this letter finds you in a better way than when
we last parted. Bitter words were exchanged. You had
taken too much liquor and we both know what that makes
you become. But I am not writing to harass and accuse. I
am writing to apologize. I was heartbroken seeing what
had become of my little girl, and what she is doing to
herself. You are destroying your body and your soul with
liquor, Evelyn, and it is harder for me to watch than you
can imagine.

11. EVELYN SUMMERS'S LETTER FROM HER MOTHER. *L.A. NOIRE.*

death. Evelyn's mother defines her daughter as having an "illness" that
needed treatment at a clinic, but would Evelyn have agreed? Players will
never know, since Evelyn is the object of narration but not the agent of
her own story. Letters as a narrative device offer a means to supply insight
into the inner thoughts, desires, and consciousness of a character, but in
this case players get to know Evelyn through her mother, a position of high
ethos; Evelyn was pathological and had caused her mother great pain. This
sentimental exercise positions Evelyn's mother as the progenitor of proper
white womanhood who seeks to reform those who do not make the transition from being single to married and, therefore, whole.

Another indicator of Evelyn's failure is her infatuation with Grosvenor.
Players learn that he has a general disdain for Evelyn and worse is a unionist
who has been arrested for inciting a labor uprising. From his ascot to his
smarmy smile, he makes labor unionists look like affected dandy intellectuals.

If Hollywood noir, particularly the hard-boiled variety, is designed to
show the grimy underbelly of the urban frontier, then what does it mean
when that underbelly comprises labor activists and intellectuals? Are these
reformers the "disease" that threatens to destroy civilization? In part, yes,
according to the game's philosophy. Grosvenor's belief in the redistribu-
tion of wealth through socialist means counters the neoliberal belief that

12. GROSVENOR MCCAFFREY. *L.A. NOIRE.*

"human rights and equality . . . are the rights and equality to compete."[36] Both Evelyn and Grosvenor are represented as queering the American way of life by refusing to conform to both the intimate public sphere of marriage and the political public sphere of unfettered capitalism. By no means am I saying that the game should support socialism. My point is that socialism is linked to degraded performances of masculinity and femininity on the homicide desk. In *L.A. Noire*, the American way of life is a capitalist enterprise in which white middle-class folk are married, buy homes, accumulate, and procreate.

Celine and Evelyn make the case for how cisgender, straight, white women should behave as members of a certain race and class level. They are also representative of whiteness itself; they are supposed to be symbols of racial and sexual purity.[37] Antonia Maldonado, the only woman of color in the game, defines the "supremacy" of white identity through her coding as a stereotypical Latina, who is working class and sexualized.[38] The investigation follows the usual pattern, where Donnelly sends Phelps out to investigate the crime. The only difference is the way he describes her, as the "poor Hispanic woman . . . murdered near City Hall and left lying naked in an alleyway." She is the only victim to be referenced by race (and also as naked). The other victims are not described as white and naked, which

13. ANTONIA MALDONADO'S BODY. *L.A. NOIRE.*

renders "white" as not only the default identity but also the identity for which privacy is respected, at least in public spheres. When players arrive on the scene, her brown skin sets her in opposition to the near-glowing whiteness of the other victims.

Maldonado's working-class status is defined by her need to live in a boarding house as opposed to the majority of white victims, who live in single dwelling houses. However, she and the other victims do share a clear relationship: the night of her death she was drinking heavily and carousing, and like the others, she pays dearly for her "selfish unwomanly fantasies of . . . sexual autonomy."[39]

Players participate in Phelps's controls of Antonia's story through his white male gaze.[40] Nowhere is Phelps's white male gaze more controlling and dominating than when he explains to Galloway why Antonia's husband, Angel Christopher Maldonado, is behaving in a violent manner: He is "a young Latino man; [the divorce] would hurt his sense of who he is. He sees himself as a failure—a woman taking control over his life." Phelps, as the detective figure, seems to engage ethnographic practice in a reasonable logical manner, but he positions both Antonia and Angel as subjects of study rather than as citizens suffering unimaginable tragedy. As a detective unraveling a mystery, players expect Phelps to explain facts, turning chaos into order through scientific, systematic analysis common in the police procedural noir thriller.[41] However, Phelps's causal connection of cultural stereotype to criminal behaviors is a logical fallacy.

Angel's Latino masculinity is set in binary opposition to Phelps's and even Galloway's white masculinity, but what of Antonia? Her role in the game story reveals just how far Celine, Evelyn, and Theresa had strayed from their position as white women. As Berlant explains, there is an obsession in American culture to cleanse the nation of "non-normal populations—immigrant, gay, sexually non-conjugal, poor, Hispanic, African Americans—from the fantasy scene of private, protected, and sanctified 'American' life," which white women are supposed to signify.[42] Antonia, as the stereotypical Latina, provides a racial and gendered measure of how far these wives and mothers have strayed from their role as the nation's moral core, which has been given sentimental ethos by Evelyn's mother. They are exposed as a social and moral problem and are "contained" violently.

The final case I want to discuss is an outlier from the other cases but still firmly ensconced within the gender norms Hollywood noir tends to police. Diedre Moller's murder is tied to ideologies of consumption and accumulation not only because she ruined her husband's life by overspending, but because, players learn, her killer collects jewelry from his victims. The murderer's collecting of objects provides an interesting and perhaps disturbing parallel to our own role as player or "interactor," to use Janet Murray's terminology. Players progress through the game by accumulating collectibles, virtual things such as suits, clues, newspapers, and golden records that can provide players with information or give extra "powers" in the game or achievement awards. When players collect everyday objects in a game that imbue their avatars with powers, players are actually interacting with "the ideological and ideational effects of the material world and transformations of it."[43]

Slavoj Žižek may not hold the intellectual stardom he once did, but he makes a good point when he notes that everyday objects can become objects of desire when the object is worth much more than its use value; it can become desire itself.[44] In a game reward system, the objects accumulated give players ideological effects, such as clothing that can be worn to fulfill public forms of performance (e.g., Phelps's array of suits that offer special abilities). Each of the five female victims (six, if Elizabeth Short is included) on the homicide desk has a fetishized totem of femininity stolen or "collected" from her body, such as Antonia's cross pendant, Theresa's white high-heeled shoe, and Celine's ring. These belongings are not simply things but are a crucial identifying feature of each victim: Antonia's religious pendant defines her sullied piety, Theresa's high-heeled shoe (her favorite pair, according to her husband) is connected to her love of dancing, and so forth. Collecting objects is a game convention, but how the rewards, objects, and clues are collected and who controls them is all about power and control.

Ian Bogost provides one of the more lengthy analyses of reward systems in his discussion of the popular sim game *Animal Crossing*, a seemingly innocuous game that is anything but: the game makes arguments about debt, consumerism, and homeownership as players build houses and buy goods for their avatars in this virtual marketplace. Christopher Paul explores the reward systems of the massively multiplayer online role-playing game *World of Warcraft*, with a focus on the controversy surrounding how certain reward systems are valued and devalued. In *L.A. Noire* players can collect suits and their abilities, clues and intuition points, Los Angeles landmarks, and achievement awards for completing certain missions or collections. They can view how many points they have accumulated and earn rewards for avatars or trophies, depending on the gaming console. Therefore, Deidre Moller's case operates as an insightful metanarrative of our own acts of accumulation as players in this game world.

Much as Elizabeth Short was reduced to the flower she wore in her hair, these virtual victims are reduced to a metonymic chain of national meaning that identifies them as valuable "things" in the American cultural field. However, is this all there is to say? It's not simply the conflation of the woman with the material object, but what about the "thingness" of the object taken? For example, what about the butterfly brooch that is taken from Deidre Moller's body or the wedding rings and other jewelry stolen from the victims? Theorists, including Arjun Appadurai and Bill Brown, have made it clear that identity in Western cultures is predicated and shaped by a relationship to possessions; therefore, the type of possession is crucial to understanding the ideologies the object narrates to the player.[45]

Let's turn to how the Hollywood noir queers our relationship to things. Much as in John Huston's *The Maltese Falcon* (1941), each case Phelps investigates on the homicide desk is named after the object taken from the victims. For example, the golden butterfly from the Moller case is an object of desire akin to the falcon; its actual functionality or sensorial value is of no consequence. While Sam Spade ties up all the narrative loose ends by the end of *The Maltese Falcon*, the falcon itself remains a lost object of desire: to solve the mystery of the falcon is to solve the root of desire, for which there is no solution, but this is not the case in *L.A. Noire*. The meaning of Diedre's butterfly brooch is anchored to her husband, Hugo Moller: he claims that his wife was a spendthrift, which players learn through, again, correct choices made in interrogation gameplay. Their run-down house is evidence of her squandering household capital on "idols" like the golden butterfly, which presumably increased her cultural and social capital. The golden butterfly, much like insurance policies and Maltese falcons, is not simply a symbol of rampant consumerism but expresses ideological desires, such as to appear to be of a different economic and social class. However, players can only assume that Deidre was the source of the family's suffering through her worship of a golden idol because she is dead: her husband and Phelps speak for her.

The use of the word "golden" pins the idea of idolatry to the butterfly brooch, which furthers the argument that Deidre's idolatry was misplaced. The procedural rhetoric of the game argues that the correct channel, conduit, or circuit for her desire was her family, which she rejected in favor of the "golden idol," so to speak. Like the other victims, her wedding ring, the sign of her legitimacy as a white middle-class woman, is ripped from her hand. This brutal act binds these women to national expectations of behavior. Their punishment for their transgression outside the bounds of middle-class domesticity is rape, mutilation, and murder.

The distinction is clear: players, as Phelps or Kelso, collect things such as suits and newspapers, which provide information or special abilities. However, objects are also collected from the bodies of the five female murder victims Phelps investigates, yet these objects hold rewards only for the male serial killer and are symbolic of their transgressive femininity. The masculine objects collected have value in a public market (e.g., suits or achievement awards); the female fetishized totems the killer collects hold value only for him, which means that the game's reward system reinforces the patriarchal ideology that women are passive objects of consumption and men are active consumers of objects. This paradigm is not surprising, claims John Sanbonmatsu, who argues that game worlds overwhelmingly "condition us into an aggressive, socially destructive form of consciousness."[46]

I have to wonder what a noir game world might be like if Marvel's acerbic, alcoholic, promiscuous hard-boiled detective, Jessica Jones, were the hero? What about Marvel's Captain America spin-off, police procedural thriller *Agent Carter*, set in the late 1940s? Carter investigates crimes, uncovers corruption, and fights misogyny. What if she were a woman of color rather than white? Noir as a genre is remarkably pliable and flexible, so much so that critics have trouble defining the genre within strict parameters. *L.A. Noire* uses the power of genre expectation and conventions to direct gameplay, which on the homicide desk reinforces rape culture, American domesticity, and patriarchal norms and value. But it didn't have to.

6 Burning Down the House

Murder, Corruption, and the Middle Class

Homeownership as a rite of passage into the American middle class seems to be a thing of the past. A quick look at the tumultuous U.S. housing market tells the story. The rate of homeownership has fallen flat or decreased since 2017, particularly in urban areas. A mere nine years earlier, the 2008 collapse caused mass foreclosures the likes of which have not been seen since the Great Depression. Henry Giroux has long argued that the United States is moving from upward mobility to downward mobility, building a permanent underclass.[1] Giroux's claims are supported by the U.S. Census, which reported in 2016 that despite the claims of economic recovery from the 2008 collapse, poverty increased in a third of U.S. counties and only 4 percent of counties reported a decline in poverty. Further, massive foreclosures resulting from the economic collapse meant that many Americans lost the base of their household wealth.[2] Sociologist Kevin Gotham writes that real estate in the United States has become "disembedded" from local conditions and now serves as a global commodity, which has created volatility in local markets.[3] In other words, real estate has transitioned into more of a commodity traded on the free market and less of an achievable signifier of success defining middle-class America. *L.A. Noire* investigates and even responds to this volatility (and related class disruptions) and, as any tough thriller must do, exposes the culprits.[4]

Much like John Marston's desire to be a landowning farmer in *Red Dead Redemption*, returning GIs in *L.A. Noire* simply want a slice of the good life they were promised. The signs of this possible middle-class life are advertised on billboards throughout the game. *L.A. Noire* quite literally deconstructs key components of the American Dream, including "upward mobility, equality, homeownership[,] ... free enterprise, and personal liberty."[5] White middle-class families are represented as both victims and perpetrators of their own demise. The only character who comes out ahead is the hard-boiled detective, Jack Kelso, who follows the pattern for cisgender, straight, white male heroes in gaming as "the only one who is above and outside the system."[6]

Hard-boiled or "tough" thrillers turned the classical detective into the ruggedly masculine (white) hero, such as Kelso, comparable to the "assertive, masculine figures of self-appointed authority" in the Western. As such, tough thrillers are particularly suited to game worlds because of the predilection in gaming to make white male player characters the default.[7] Head writer Brendan McNamara uses the capacity of open-world games to "remix" the conventions of a variety of tough thrillers, creating an environment where the hard-boiled detective and the police detective, the femme fatale, gangsters, and other figures from noir subgenres can interact via multiple, yet interconnected, storylines. This type of genre remixing in game worlds, to build on Michelle Knobel's and Colin Lankshear's thinking about digital remixing, expands the narrative possibilities for the tough thriller. However, while Knobel and Lankshear argue that digital remixing creates something new (bringing to mind the modernist call to "make it new"), this isn't fully the case when durable literary genres meet video games.[8] The print and film conventions of a ruggedly masculine detective, which help to define what makes a man on the urban frontier, is expressed in new ways via the ability of game worlds to orchestrate multiple genre types (and conventions and stock characters) into cohesive, interactive, and performative narratives. Through this tough thriller game world, the player comes to understand not only what makes the American man and wrecks the American family but also what corrupted the dream of home-ownership and all it implies.

This playable bricolage of noir conventions includes a form of Hollywood film noir popular in the late 1940s that focused on class disruption and resistance. Dennis Broe provides an overview of the rather leftist ideals that informed Hollywood noir in this period, including the belief that economic precarity and inequality was not the fault of the working or middle class but of a parasitic class that "feasted off their labor and often arranged events to make these classes appear to be guilty." This definition of film noir in this period certainly describes part of the main plotline in *L.A. Noire* where corporate fat cats, political elite, law enforcement, and real estate moguls conspire to bilk war veterans out of their property. So, then, is *L.A. Noire* part of this popular form of noir where audiences are encouraged to sympathize with the fugitive protagonist who tries to win a rigged game. Sure, former field medic Courtney Sheldon, who steals army-issue morphine to sell for profit and in turn share the wealth with his returning unit, might seem like an ideal fugitive protagonist, but he is not a player character. Therefore, his influence is limited by his lack of playability, and, further, his plan has a large body count due to numerous overdoses. Sheldon doesn't warrant sympathy, which indicates that the arson desk (in this last part of the game) is a form of the police procedural where the "fugitive is now seen as a psychotic menace."9

As an aside, Sheldon is not the psychotic menace; rather, he is a patsy for the parasitic class. A mentally ill friend from his unit, Ira Hogeboom, is the "psychotic menace." More on this later in the chapter. What I've outlined here is not simply an interesting background to the *L.A. Noire* plotline, but the genre conventions that are game constants—rules the developers need to follow to meet genre expectations. Players must follow the game mechanics, such as finding clues (to expose greedy homeowners), interrogations (to uncover corruption), and shooting and fighting (to capture suspects and defend the innocent). These are part of the procedural rhetoric of the game, which are dependent on genre conventions that organize the gameplay into a coherent, cohesive narrative that enforces certain ideologies.

L.A. Noire argues that homeownership was a fraudulent dream from the beginning with a plotline that culminates in the serial deaths of middle-class families through arson. The game responds to continuing economic precariousness and disparity in the United States, paralleling the conditions that produced American forms of noir in the 1940s, except that noir in the 1940s was form of cinema usually set in its time period. *L.A. Noire* is a nostalgic remediation of Hollywood noir set in 1947. By rewriting American postwar prosperity as a historical myth, the real-life decline of the American middle class is given an origin story. Both *L.A. Noire* and *Red Dead Redemption* follow in the footsteps of their print and film ancestors, persuading players that the best form of upward mobility, if any is to be had, embraces the extreme individualism of the rugged frontier spirit, embodied and made playable through Kelso, whose moral code includes pulling himself up by the bootstraps and being self-sufficient.

The central and subplots in *L.A. Noire* owe a debt to noir films like William Wyler's *Desperate Hours* (1955), in which an escaped convict terrorizes a middle-class family, and Billy Wilder's *Double Indemnity* (1944), in which the happy housewife/femme fatale manipulates an insurance salesman to murder her husband.[10] Tough thrillers reveal that temptation, death, and destruction lurk just around the corner in American suburbia. By setting the game in 1947, when suburbia was burgeoning, McNamara creates an origin story for the tragic end of the American middle class in the twenty-first century. In *L.A. Noire*, suburbia is a fraud: the houses are built from old movie sets; homes are burned down (with families in them) so wealthy white men can profit from the insurance. If suburbia is the visual image of the American Dream itself—"the promised land of the American middle class"—then *L.A. Noire* destroys suburbia and in tandem the middle class.[11] Through a realistic, historical setting where players can interact with historical figures, such as Mickey Cohen and Johnny Stompanato, *L.A. Noire* makes the claim that the American middle class was doomed from the beginning.

Playing with History

The nostalgic temporal setting of *L.A. Noire* is significant. Alison Landsberg explains that our actual relationship to historical events and figures has become so mediated that we cannot distinguish between what is real (can be traced to an origin) and what is hyperreal (models of the real with no origin).[12] In a sense, *L.A. Noire* is simulacra of simulacra. American noir grew directly out of the crime film, which dramatized real-life criminal events.[13] Since the player experiences this genre with its "historically accurate" elements as gameplay, it seems real. Landsberg explains this phenomenon through what she calls "experiential museums," such as the United States Holocaust Memorial Museum, that allow people "the collective opportunity of having an experiential relationship to a collective and cultural past that they did not experience." Through the embodied, haptic experience of gameplay, players are equally invited to "experience history in a personal and even bodily way."[14] A number of games incorporate experiential history via gameplay but perhaps none more famously and more celebrated than the *Assassin's Creed* franchise, which works hard to give veracity to the prosthetic memories it supplies players (through explanations of the time period, buildings, and other game elements supplied outside gameplay in a menu option). In *L.A. Noire*, when players experience the game world via Kelso, they in turn have an experiential relationship that seems real. In the case of the Holocaust museum, the point of such an experiential relationship has an ethical imperative, creating a connection with victims and their histories to ensure such a genocide does not happen again. However, the flip side of such experiential relationships to historical events and figures is the manipulation of the audience's very perception of reality.

This kind of historical experience, explains Claudio Fogu, changes our relationship to temporality itself. Video games (and even other multimodal forms of experiencing history) spatialize history, detaching it from its referential anchors and therefore changing its meaning by eliminating representation. Because we are immersed within a historical time and place and often interacting with historical characters, players are not understanding an event or figure as something or someone of the past but are instead immersed in what *may* happen.[15] History, then, becomes a causal factor of what lies ahead rather than a reflection on what came before. *L.A. Noire*, therefore, is an apparently realistic space of historical possibility directed by noir conventions, such as anxieties over middle-class decline, rampant corporate corruption, and straitlaced tough-guy investigators.[16]

The Destruction of the Suburban Frontier

The majority of the final missions of the game, which are located on the arson desk, are spent driving through tracts of partially developed land that are a barren and deadly (sub)urban frontier. Hal Himmelstein defines the popular myth of suburbia as a utopic space set between the frontier wilderness and urban squalor. In *L.A. Noire*, suburbia comprises half-built homes for returning veterans.[17] There are aspects of *L.A. Noire* that can be effectively paralleled with the social anxieties that frontier narratives tried to quell. Suburbia as the promised land in the game seems descended from the nineteenth-century depiction of the frontier as a safety valve for growing tensions in the urban squalor of the great eastern cities.[18] Similarly, the American suburb was a cultural symbol of "refuge from the effects of urbanization" in the twentieth century.[19] However, the common depiction of suburbia as a refuge from urban life has transitioned in contemporary popular culture to the American suburb as a gothic space in which "the most dangerous threats come from within, not from without." A space where everything that's wrong with American society is mirrored—from mindless accumulation to zombie-like conventionality—suburbia is disturbia in twenty-first-century popular culture.[20]

What sets *L.A. Noire* apart from suburban gothic games—such as Pandemic's darkly satirical *Destroy All Humans* (2005)—is that suburbia is seen not in its antithetical form as "homogenized, soulless, plastic landscape of tepid conformity" but either as an unfinished (sub)urban frontier of failed possibility or a space of murder and destruction.[21] The suburbs in *L.A. Noire* are poorly built and made to be destroyed for profit. Much like the false promise of the original frontier, where settlers were lured by promises of the good life, this frontier is not built to house the dreams of the masses, but to fill the pockets of the few. This frontier paradigm is taken up by

Hollywood noir in the postwar period, revealing an ideological continuity in how land ownership is often seen a means to escape precarity but is rarely so in reality.[22] The nightmare of this suburbia is not conformity or slavish consumption but its destruction through the greed of the elite, against whom even the police detective and hard-boiled detective are almost helpless. Neither Phelps's intellect and liberal rationality nor Kelso's frontiersman manliness and preternatural know-how can save anyone, except the failed femme fatale, the captive damsel in distress, Elsa Lichtmann.

Back in chapter 4, I argued that the game's ostensible protagonist, Phelps, embodies classic liberalism in that he believes in the power of intellect, rationality, and law and order. By the end of the game, Phelps's liberal, Jeffersonian ideals are in ruins, much like the surburbia he swore to protect. Players are first introduced to Phelps in his beat uniform, leaving his suburban home and waving goodbye to his wife and kids. By the final chapters of the game, Phelps has been evicted from the good life for committing adultery with the hapless Elsa Lichtmann. Phelps redeems himself through self-sacrifice by saving her, killing the psychotic fugitive stock character Hogeboom, and then dying tragically. Does his death perpetuate the idea that the trappings of the American middle class, such as property ownership, heterosexual marriage, and accumulation, are worth dying for?

I don't have a clear answer, but what I do know is that *L.A. Noire* offers players limited and even rigid choices that follow the often bleak options characters face in tough thrillers. Players are encouraged to believe they are powerless to stop corruption. There is little accumulation of wealth or privilege in the game—players can drive hidden cars and gain outfits for Phelps to wear by increasing their rank (achieved through correctly assessed interrogations and clue detection), but unlike in the *Grand Theft Auto* series, wealth can't be accumulated. In the end, Assistant District Attorney Leonard Petersen makes a side deal to prosecute only two of the seven insurance fraud perpetrators, one of whom is dead. Government officials, law enforcement, and other community leaders are left to presumably continue their corrupt activities. This plot is reminiscent of the famous line from Roman Polanski's 1974 classic neo-noir thriller, *Chinatown*, when the main character Jake Gittes is told, "Forget it, Jake, it's Chinatown." There is no fighting corruption, so grin and bear it. This kind of nihilism is a common feature of noir as a whole.[23]

Throughout the game, players follow the plotline of fraud and arson through cutscenes, which appear once the player picks up a newspaper (discussed in more detail in chapter 4). The point of convergence between the gaming plotline and the newspaper cutscenes is imminent when Sheldon, the army medic who had served under Phelps and Kelso, confides in his therapist, Harlan Fontaine, who is in on the fraud, about the morphine heist he and his fellow veterans committed. Sheldon is also in trouble with mobsters who want in on the morphine scam. Sheldon doesn't turn to Phelps but Kelso, who takes over as player character for several cases on the arson desk. He is the dominant character despite appearing at the end of the game. A quick search of discussions on Reddit and other message boards reveals Kelso's popularity.[24] Phelps doesn't fare as well, with players expressing dissatisfaction with him over the course of the game.[25] Kelso's primary purpose in the game is to serve as a nihilistic example of how to deal with the collapse of the American Dream, which in turn allows the profit-hungry, greedy neoliberal characters (e.g., members of the Suburban Redevelopment Fund) to continue accumulating.

Burning Down the House: The Arson Desk Cases

On the arson desk, Phelps comes full circle, from investigating the robbery of private property at the opening of the game to investigating the destruction of private property by fire at the end of the game. The entire game threads this main plotline throughout. What game worlds do that films and novels can't (except experimentally) is create a narrative that enables the audience to move in and out of a storyline multiple times without losing or destabilizing the audience to the point of disconnection from the narrative (admittedly, certain forms of literature desire this effect). Right from the first case, when Phelps is a patrolman, the collectible newspapers start to unfold the main storyline, which is fully realized over the course of the arson desk cases. As the player finds more papers (thirteen in total), more of the main plot is revealed. These newspaper cutscenes may have been inspired by Robert Siodmak's *The Killers* (1946), in which the background of a heist is revealed by a narrator reading the news story about it out loud while the camera zooms in to the photo of the heist and, in turn, to a flashback sequence (though revealing information via newspapers is a common film device in the twentieth century).[26] It's unlikely that viewers would put up with a character picking up thirteen newspapers to reveal scenes of parallel action over the course of a two-hour film. *L.A. Noire* combines a rewards system based on repetition and goal-oriented behavior with film conventions to unravel the plot, at once creating narrative cohesion and reinforcing the game's arguments about property and class. The newspapers throughout the game uncover the criminal underbelly of real estate and land development in Los Angeles, which become playable cases on the arson desk.

The first case on the arson desk, titled "The Gas Man," involves the Suburban Redevelopment Fund, a committee of powerful community leaders dedicated to the development of homes for returning GIs. This committee is corrupt, buying out homeowners to develop fraudulent homes. Families who don't sell their homes to the Suburban Redevelopment Fund are given a "free" vacation to Catalina Island overnight, and when they return their homes have been burned to the ground. This scam fails horribly when the Sawyers, who did not use their free trip, die in their beds of smoke inhalation. Other survivors of arson tell Phelps and his partner Herschel Biggs (who is also the voice-over narrator) that they were under pressure by the Suburban Redevelopment Fund to sell their homes. When they tried to hold out for a better price, their homes were destroyed by fire.

These homeowners seem to be the victims of the "parasitic class," but they are also partly implicated in their own victimhood. Seemingly small details, such as a homeowner briefly admitting to negotiating for more money, shape the ideological perspective of the narrative. The procedural rhetoric of the interrogation process persuades players that homeowners must take part of the blame. Phelps's questioning of Don Steffens, one of the homeowners under pressure to sell his house, provides a good example of this game procedure. After each question, Steffens's eyes shift back and forth, a rule-based signal that players should not trust him (he's literally shifty). Upon choosing the "doubt" option (or "bad cop" in the remastered edition), players are rewarded with "intuition points" for correctly

14. INTUITION POINTS. *L.A. NOIRE.*

identifying his attempt to cover up his deception. It bears repeating that the entire interrogation procedure is governed by the noir police procedural.

Later, we also learn that Steffens tried to manipulate InstaHeat, a fuel heating company, into providing free repairs, again defining him as a greedy man. This whole sequence could have been a cutscene, but instead the questioning of Steffens becomes part of the win-lose conditions of the game. Players' success at interrogation is evaluated by a rating out of five stars at the end of the case. If players can get Steffens to confess to his various sins, they win rewards and a higher case rating. This playable plotline draws from a long line of noir films produced in the 1940s and 1950s that dealt with middle-class struggle, including war veterans returning to a "greedy, atomized home front."[27]

Biggs and Phelps are told by the fire chief to start with the water heaters, which are made by InstaHeat. When they investigate InstaHeat, players learn from the manager, Ivan Rasic, that the water heaters in the family fires were indeed subtly tampered with, and again through interrogation gameplay, that InstaHeat is corrupt. Rasic confesses that the company sold faulty water heaters because "none of us could keep up with the amount of housing going up," but the water heaters are not "all faulty." The procedural rhetoric of the game would seem to point to corporate greed as to blame

15. GRUESOME FAMILY PORTRAIT. *L.A. NOIRE.*

here, but that assumption is dashed when Phelps and Biggs question the InstaHeat technicians, who installed the heaters.

Phelps and Biggs investigate Matthew Ryan, whose locker at InstaHeat contains pro-anarchist pamphlets. Much like the socialist activist Grosvenor McCaffrey and the hobo leader (investigated by Phelps in cases on the homicide desk), Ryan is akin to the sociopathic criminal or the "psychotic criminal" of the McCarthy-era noir, whose unpatriotic behavior threatens "the fabric of society."[28] Ryan is interrogated and roughed up for daring to resist capitalist values. Some may argue that these socialist and anarchist characters are indicative of the time period, but they are more indicative of a shift in the values and beliefs of the time period the game was produced in. Noir is a slippery genre with many facets, and the fact that McNamara and his team chose these particular forms of the noir is telling. Eventually, Ryan is exonerated of arson (but not of his belief system) only when another family is murdered.

The final family is murdered via gas asphyxiation. After the family's death, the arsonist returns to the crime scene to reposition the family in the living room together on their knees, as if praying.

Phelps deduces this arsonist also caused the Sawyer fire and through guilt arranged the bodies of this family as a way for them to be together in death. Leland Monroe, the CEO of Elysian Fields (pun intended) and a member of the Suburban Redevelopment Fund, is directly linked not only to the Sawyer family murder but also to the arson of GIs' homes. Biggs, who was reluctant to question Monroe because he is close friends with the police chief and the mayor (who are also members of the Suburban Redevelopment Fund), agrees to pursue Monroe as a suspect. The game story casts all involved, from homeowners to socialist-leaning individuals to the "parasitic class," as culpable.

There is an interesting narrative intersection between *Red Dead Redemption* and *L.A. Noire* via Monroe's interrogation sequence. Monroe explains that "progress is an inexorable process, detective. Those who choose to stand in defiance are usually confined to the waste basket of history." This philosophy is shockingly similar to that of the main villain in *Red Dead Redemption*, Agent Edgar Ross, who claims that "savages" and all others who would stand in the way of progress must be wiped out. While both characters are antagonists in their games, which would seem to be a protest against such a neoliberal point of view regarding self-sufficiency, unfettered capitalism, and rampant colonialism, it's not, because as in *Red Dead Redemption*, Monroe represents a seemingly unstoppable system. For example, while John Marston's son, Jack Marston, gets revenge for his father's death in *Red Dead Redemption* by killing Ross, it ultimately does not matter: the government will go on; neoliberal accumulation will continue; corruption is inevitable. To drive the point home even further, Jack Marston kills Edgar Ross once he's retired, after another federal officer has taken his place. The cycle continues. Similarly, in *L.A. Noire*, as Monroe says, "progress is an inexorable process." So inexorable that Phelps and Biggs are unable to solve this case.

Phelps and Biggs are clearly in over their heads. The chief of police, William Worrell, is a member of the Suburban Redevelopment Fund. This is the point in the game where Kelso takes over as the main player character because he is "the only one who is above and outside the system."[29] Even though Salter and Blodgett are defining a common white male avatar in gaming, they perhaps unwittingly are also defining the hard-boiled detective. He, like the frontiersman, has a strict moral code and can move between criminal or "savage" and civilized worlds. By returning to settings previously investigated by Phelps, such as the Elysian Fields construction site or interrogating real estate developer Leland Monroe, players are able to view the game world through two perspectives: the hard-boiled detective, Kelso, and the law-and-order police detective, Phelps. Because Kelso can solve the case where Phelps could not, Kelso is made to seem more effective.

Kelso winds up in the hospital after a particularly grueling fight with Monroe's thugs. He refuses to be nursed but instead says, "I know how to take my licks." The battered and bruised cowboy is a convention of the Western genre and is often a part of tough thrillers. From Sam Spade to Rick Deckard, the hard-boiled detective must be able to handle pain with stoicism (and sometimes a stiff drink). Even though Kelso does not stay in his convalescence for long, he is in a hospital, a female nurse by his side, and she provides the "restorative female 'gaze' at the male body . . . [that] forms the necessary catalyst to the recreation of that body."[30] The rejuvenated male body signifies that the frontier hero (whether cowboy or hard-boiled detective) has been given the blessing of white womanhood, the moral compass of the nation, to do what needs to be done to protect "civilization." Kelso leaves the hospital, determined to save Lichtmann from Monroe's men, who have been sent to kill her.

The shift to Kelso changes the procedurality of the game drastically. Kelso breaks rules (unlike Phelps) to protect "the little guy," as Kelso puts it. Kelso's moral code echoes Richard Slotkin's description of the hard-boiled detective as protecting the "little man."[31] Kelso's dominance in the game story is made clear through his negotiations with the Assistant District Attorney Petersen. Every time he tries to ask Kelso a question, Kelso responds with a question. The ability to ask questions is an indication of authority, and Kelso's refusal to respond to authority indicates he has linguistic control.[32] Phelps couldn't do this within the parameters of the game as the police detective. Kelso even takes to opportunity to tell Petersen how to do his job, referencing the shady characters Petersen deals with: "There's a problem with colorful characters. First they send you over a drink, then they buy you dinner, then you get a phone call in the middle of the night for a favor.

Try rubbing shoulders with some solid citizens—they're the ones you are supposed to protect."

Kelso assumes a level of moral authority that is above the law, so much so that when Petersen offers Kelso a job to help him take down the vice squad, Kelso refuses, directing Petersen to investigate the arson cases. Note that Kelso, unlike Phelps, does not accept reward and nor does he need to protect his family and home (he has neither). Kelso is not part of the system, echoing his forebears, Hawkeye, Daniel Boone, Sam Spade, and others. For Kelso, whatever the vice squad is doing as a corrupt repressive state apparatus takes a backseat to the violation of American citizens, particularly war veterans who want to gain the ethos of property ownership.

Property ownership is exposed as nothing more than a fantasy. Leland Monroe, after all, is heard repeatedly on the car radio (and visually on billboards) stating that homeownership is the fulfillment of the American Dream. However, this dream is shown to be as fabricated as the old movie sets that supplied the building materials. While the corruption may be made more apparent in *L.A. Noire*, the job of the hard-boiled detective, much like the outlaw-cowboy in *Red Dead Redemption*, is clear: property ownership is for profit—it's a commodity, not a right. The solution in both games is not to rise up but to cast blame and then accept this economic reality as the norm.

Homeowners are as greedy as the members of the Suburban Redevelopment Fund. The "good life" is costly, and most noir protagonists realize that they will never have access to the brass ring.[33] In *L.A. Noire*, however, it's not a matter of the hard-boiled detective recognizing his exclusion from the "good life" but rather of American citizens as a whole simply being undeserving of the good life. War veterans steal and commit murder, middle-class Americans are greedy, and the elite are corrupt. The only person who is without "sin" is Kelso, who tells his former boss, Curtis Benson, the head of California Fire and Life and, of course, also a member of the Suburban Redevelopment Fund, that he is not worried by threats from the elite because "my California is different from your California."

When Kelso exposes the Suburban Redevelopment Fund members' plot to subvert and destroy suburbia, players are not witnessing a grand resistance but a means to reconcile the player with the realities of a post-collapse world. In the neoliberal landscape of the game, anarchists, labor leaders, and anyone else who stands in the way of free-market enterprise and profit must be jailed or killed. Similar to the corporate interests and neoliberal governmentality in *Red Dead Redemption*, the corporate interests and corrupt public officials in *L.A. Noire* face few repercussions. Nowhere does this paradigm become more apparent than the closing scenes of the game, which involve Kelso invading Monroe's mansion with his former band of brothers.

Kelso traps Monroe in his office, where Monroe tells him that the housing development and insurance scam cannot be stopped at this late stage. Kelso answers, "Kingdoms rise and kingdoms fall; ask the Emperor of Japan." Kelso then keeps his word (a hard-boiled detective's word is bond), shooting Monroe in the legs. Kelso identifies Monroe as a "savage" enemy of the United States and neutralizes him without mercy. There is no middle ground in this urban frontier: there are friend and enemies, no in-between. Even when Kelso learns from Monroe that the arsonist burning down houses is one of Phelps's former men, the cowboy Ira Hogeboom, Kelso ends up killing him as well: Hogeboom is identified as the psychotic criminal who threatens the fabric of society, but does he really?

Traumatized by the war, particularly by Phelps's inept leadership, Hogeboom is manipulated by his psychiatrist, Fontaine (also a member of the Suburban Redevelopment Fund), to commit arson, but when he finds out that he has been manipulated and has killed families, he seeks revenge. Hogeboom burns down the houses the Suburban Redevelopment Fund needed to keep in order to prove that the other fires were "accidental." Then Hogeboom takes revenge on his therapist, murdering Fontaine and taking Elsa Lichtmann, also a patient of Fontaine's, hostage. This is a far cry from the gentle cowboy revealed via flashbacks of the war shown before each case (yet another storyline).

Hogeboom was a cowboy laborer before the war, but Phelps ordered him to use a flamethrower to clear out a suspected Japanese cell, only to discover that he had slaughtered innocent civilians. As Mark Osteen explains, "noir vets" usually have a specific narrative function, to "expose a cultural yearning to punish and then redeem, in which hope for restitution collides with profound anxieties about disability and memory as threats to the stability of the society and the psyche."[34] Hogeboom is certainly framed as a threat to the stability of both economic progress and white masculinity. As the cowboy figure, Hogeboom could not navigate the urban frontier. He is an overlapping site of national discourses and tensions that goes wildly out of control. He is the savage who has captured a white woman (or "princess," as Kelso calls all women in the game, a particularly annoying habit). His disruption of the narrative serves to define a "real man" as embodied by Kelso, but he also serves as Phelps's reckoning. Both Hogeboom and Phelps are ruthlessly removed from the urban frontier.

Kelso is certainly a figure of nihilistic libertarianism, dismissing the rule of law as a solution to corruption. Phelps tells Kelso that he needs Hogeboom alive to testify against the Suburban Redevelopment Fund members. Kelso's response either suggests he is in on the corruption or he is, like many white male player characters, "above the system and outside of it."[35] To Kelso, Hogeboom is a national liability, damaged beyond repair. Kelso asks Phelps, "hasn't this man done enough for you?" referring to Hogeboom's taking the fall for Phelps's ineptitude as a commander in the war. This question again positions Kelso as in linguistic control and in turn blames Phelps for Hogeboom's crimes. Despite Phelps's reasonable request to protect Hogeboom as a material witness, Kelso shoots Hogeboom to apparently "put him out of his misery." Kelso lives in the either-or geography of the frontier. There is no space of ambiguity or difference. Hogeboom was a damaged man, whose life, Kelso surmised, was not worth living. He had not only transgressed his rugged individualism but "went savage" by kidnapping Lichtmann, who may be a German immigrant but has shown her worth through Kelso's admiration for her subservience to his wishes and her resistance to Phelps.

In an act of self-sacrificial redemption, Phelps saves Lichtmann and Kelso before being swept away by a flash flood in the river tunnel system. At Phelps's funeral, Roy Earle, Phelps's partner who double-crossed him, ironically gives the eulogy, thanking Phelps for bringing down Monroe and the "evil" Dr. Fontaine. Earle praises Phelps as a good husband and father, therefore rewriting his narrative to fit the parameters of the American Dream, sustaining it as myth: Phelps was a heroic man who served the state well—a good husband, father, and homeowner. In death, Phelps becomes a sentimental figure of American prosperity rather than a flawed human being who was valued and loved. The game certainly uses irony to critique the American Dream, but Kelso as the last moral (white) man standing sends a powerful message to players: a good (white male) citizen is not one who upholds the law and exposes corruption, trying to make the world a better place. There are no good citizens left because every facet of the world is corrupt and filled with conspiracies. *L.A. Noire* is more than bleak; it forecloses on alternative ways of being and understanding the world. If everyone is greedy and self-serving, then no one is worth saving, leaving the cisgender, straight, white male hard-boiled detective as the "idealised and undivided figure of masculine potency and invulnerability."[36]

Afterword

Tom Stoppard makes an excellent point about the power of genres in *Rosencrantz and Guildenstern Are Dead* through The Player, who explains, "The audience knows what to expect and it's all they are prepared to believe in."[1] Genres can be pliable to an extent, but as Stoppard notes, these expectations "are all [the audience] are prepared to believe in." It's the implications of this phrase that cause concern. If audiences have set expectations regarding how a Western or a hard-boiled thriller operates, then that belief can be strong enough to forgive (and hopefully not celebrate) racism, misogyny, colonialism, white triumphalism, and other inequalities and oppressions endemic to these genres. An example of implementing the modern Western uncritically is the unmitigated slaughter of "Indians" in *Red Dead Redemption*. Considering the history of genocidal acts by the United States and Canada perpetuated against Indigenous peoples, I was horrified that this kind of gameplay was not only encouraged but rewarded. How did Dan Houser, head writer and co-founder of Rockstar Games, get away with making genocide playable?[2] Because this game is a Western, and cowboys killing "savages" is a genre convention. But it doesn't have to be.

Genres matter. They are dynamic and tell us what's required of us in any given social situation. Much like an interface that provides certain affordances and capacity for interaction within a defined framework, genres frame most, if not all, rhetorical and social situations. When do we speak? How should we speak? What's the acceptable vocabulary in a particular rhetorical situation? If you've ever misjudged the genre and said something unsuitable, then you've felt the social censure. Literary genres, akin to genres of communication, also teach us how to deal with rhetorical and social situations, perhaps even more profoundly than everyday communication genres. For Kenneth Burke, all stories have some relationship to parables: they teach us lessons and, in turn, give us equipment for living.[3] However, in games studies, genres are still largely thought of as categories. They are a means to group forms of gameplay, as evidenced by the myriad journal articles and books that argue how games should be classified rather than investigating how literary genres direct the diegesis and procedural rhetoric of game worlds.

One of the reasons I felt compelled to write this book is that game worlds bring the conventions of durable literary genres to life. I don't mean "to life" in terms of positivity jingoism but more in the sense of Frankenstein's creature. Durable literary genres have birthed damaging, poisonous stereotypes, such as the Noble Native, (white) hypermasculinity, and damsels in distress. But again, they don't have to. Game worlds powerfully influence the ways in which players process information; therefore, when game worlds are powered by durable literary genres, logically, their persuasive power increases. Because video games can encode and digitize objects, interactions, bodies, and so forth from the real world, these stereotypes can either be reborn or their fundamental DNA transformed.[4] In other words, do we have to play as John Marston or Jack Kelso? There are lots of revisionist Westerns and hard-boiled thrillers out there. Stories can heal or stories can poison, and both the media and genre matter in terms of just how healing or poisonous a story might be.

Therefore, remediating durable literary genres into game worlds should not be enacted uncritically, yet it consistently is. This uncritical remediation is what inspired the subtitle of this book, "Genre Trouble." Game worlds have genre trouble when conventions of the frontier Western and hard-boiled noir are remediated without addressing the inequalities built into these genres, such as white supremacy and misogyny. I certainly didn't come up with these arguments. There's rafts of research about the ways the frontier Western and hard-boiled noir perpetuated forms of cisgender, straight, white masculinity that worked to contain and neutralize "savagery" of all kinds (from "Indians" to anarchists).

Noir and Western literature scholars, including Dennis Broe, Joan Copjec, Frank Krutnik, Christine Bold, Richard Slotkin, Louis Owens, and Victoria Lamont, have extensively mapped the troublesome topography of these genres. The power and origin of these durable genres in print and film media is indisputable at this point. As demonstrated by texts from Richard Slotkin's triptych on the origins and development of the Western and hard-boiled noir to Christine Bold's exposé of the print history of the frontier Western, these genres have had a profound effect on how the United States views itself as a nation and how its viewed internationally. This vast body of work should not be siloed but facilitate the study of how these genres are remediated into digital forms. The type of genre analysis I conducted in this book is only the tip of the iceberg.

I hope this book influences how you view game stories powered by literary genres. It's become something of a commonplace to include a call to action in critiques of game-world inequalities. Shira Chess, Megan Condis, and many other game scholars call for greater diversity in gaming, often asking developers to create more inclusive games. There is no authorless literature in massive game worlds, just executive writers, like Dan Houser and Brendan McNamara (of the now-defunct Team Bondi), who control the means of production. It's highly unlikely that developers, with their precarious work environments, might want to suggest a drastic change to a generic formula that has sold millions of games. As well as asking "game creators, game players, and game researchers" to make games more diverse in terms of gender, race, sexuality, and even objectives, I'd like to add higher education to the list. I'm singling out the humanities, in particular, which desperately needs to reassess what's considered acceptable material for study.[5] Perhaps it's time to move beyond the academic comfort zones of print and film media and venture into the game worlds that are helping to shape the world we live in.

NOTES

INTRODUCTION

1. When I use the word "literary" in this book, I'm including the most common legacy media that these genres have told stories through: print and film. The word "literary" is really a term of value more than a definition of medium.
2. Bogost, *Unit Operations*, 13.
3. "Hollywood noir" most often refers to noir produced by major American film studios in the 1940s and 1950s.
4. Bogost, *Persuasive Games*, 14.
5. Juul, *Half-Real Video Games*, 5, 73.
6. Goldberg, *All Your Base Are Belong to Us*.
7. Howells, "Watching a Game, Playing a Movie."
8. Neale, *Genre and Hollywood*, 26.
9. Derrida, *Acts of Literature*, 225.
10. Fay and Nieland, *Film Noir*, 125.
11. Miller, "Genre as Social Action."
12. Devitt, *Writing Genres*, 14.
13. Miller, "Genre as Social Action," 162–65.
14. Galloway, *Gaming*, 128n8.
15. Galloway, *Gaming*, 1.
16. Wolf, "Genre and the Video Game."
17. Wolf, "Genre and the Video Game," 115.
18. Galloway, *Gaming*, 128.

19. Neale, *Genre and Hollywood*, 16.

20. Eskelinen, "The Gaming Situation."

21. King and Krzywinska, *ScreenPlay*, 2, 26–27.

22. Clearwater, "What Defines a Video Game Genre"; Apperley, "Genre and Game Studies."

23. Bold, *The Frontier Club*, xx.

24. Cawelti, *The Six-Gun Mystique*, 2, 72.

25. Tompkins, *West of Everything*, 62.

26. Slotkin, *Gunfighter Nation*, 175.

27. Tatum and Graulich, *Reading* The Virginian *in the New West*.

28. Bold, *The Frontier Club*, 2.

29. Bold, "Westerns," 327.

30. Bold, *The Frontier Club*, 2.

31. Bold, *The Frontier Club*, 4.

32. Humphreys, "'Truer 'n Hell,'" 33.

33. Bold, *The Frontier Club*, 8, 1.

34. Salter and Blodgett, *Toxic Geek Masculinity in Media*, 75.

35. Slotkin, *Gunfighter Nation*, 217.

36. The Pinkerton National Detective Agency (which is still open for business) served corporate interests and needs, such as violently quelling labor uprisings.

37. Slotkin, *Gunfighter Nation*, 220.

38. *Red Dead Redemption* and *L.A. Noire* are only two of many games (such as *Assassin's Creed III* and *Bioshock Infinite*) with main characters who, like any good frontiersmen, work both sides of the good-and-evil dichotomy.

39. Slotkin, *Gunfighter Nation*, 221, 175–76.

40. Harvey, *A Brief History of Neoliberalism*, 3.

41. Salter and Blodgett, *Toxic Geek Masculinity in Media*, 75, 77.

42. Rifkin, "Settler States of Feeling."

43. Yellow Bird, "What We Want to Be Called."

1. THE GAME AND THE NATION

1. Wister, *The Virginian*, 108.

2. Scharnhorst, *Owen Wister and the West*, 145.

3. Bold, *The Frontier Club*, 133.

4. Bold, *The Frontier Club*.

5. Brisbin, *The Beef Bonanza*, 17.

6. Turner, "The Frontier in American History."

7. Bold, *The Frontier Club*, xvii.

8. I follow Jack Halberstam's lead in using the term "masculinity" as a way to describe a certain set of behaviors and affects that cannot be reduced "down to the male body and its effects" (Halberstam, *Female Masculinity*, 1).

9. Pettegrew, *Brutes in Suits*, 22–23.

10. Smith, *Decolonizing Methodologies*, 20.

11. Anderson, *Cowboy Imperialism and Hollywood Film*, 7.

12. Keller, "Historical Discourse and American Identity," 240–41.

13. Belsey, "Constructing the Subject."

14. King, *The Truth about Stories*, 9.

15. Murray, *Hamlet on the Holodeck*.

16. Goldberg, *All Your Base Are Belong to Us*, 305.

17. Goldberg, *All Your Base Are Belong to Us*, 305.

18. Suellentrop, "Americana at Its Most Felonious."

19. Fisher, *Capitalist Realism*, 2, 6.

20. Wister, *The Virginian*.

21. Bal, *Double Exposures*, 4.

22. Behrenshausen, "Toward a (Kin)Aesthetic of Video Gaming," 335, 336.

23. Ricœur, *A Ricoeur Reader*.

24. Moos, *Outside America*, 2.

25. Mitchell, *Westerns*, 27.

26. Riis, *Theodore Roosevelt*, 84.

27. Mitchell, *Westerns*, 26.

28. Salter and Blodgett, *Toxic Geek Masculinity*.

29. Cheng, *Inauthentic*, 3.

30. Pettegrew, *Brutes in Suits*, 19; Salter and Blodgett, *Toxic Geek Masculinity*.

31. Lamont, "The Bovine Object of Ideology," 378, 381.

32. "States with the Highest Foreclosure Rates."

33. West, Interview, 277.

34. Žižek, *The Sublime Object of Ideology*.

35. Volkan, "Not Letting Go," 165–66.

36. Foucault, "What Is an Author?," 115.

37. Foucault, "What Is an Author?," 119.

38. Halberstam, *Female Masculinity*, 1.

39. Pettegrew, *Brutes in Suits*, 63.

40. Kaplan, "Manifest Domesticity."

41. Kolodny, *The Land before Her*.

42. Golumbia, "Games without Play," 182.

43. Golumbia, "Games without Play."

44. Golumbia, "Games without Play," 186, my italics.

45. Behrenshausen, "Toward a (Kin)Aesthetic of Video Gaming," 336.

46. Loxley, *Performativity*, 145.

47. Harvey, *A Brief History of Neoliberalism*, 7.

48. Mitchell, *Westerns*, 179.

49. Brown, "Wounded Attachments," 391.

50. Brown, "Wounded Attachments," 395.

2. MANIFEST MEMORY

1. Silko, *Ceremony*, 2.

2. Loyall, "Response," 2.

3. From here on out, I call the missions completed in Nuevo Paraiso the Mexico missions.

4. Vila, *Crossing Borders, Reinforcing Borders*, 81.

5. Please see "A Portrait of America's Middle Class, by the Numbers."

6. Bold, *The Frontier Club*.

7. Pettegrew, *Brutes in Suits*, 222.

8. Lamont, "The Bovine Object of Ideology."

9. In *Red Dead Redemption II*, released in November 2018, Marston works on a ranch and starts his homestead.

10. Kripke, "Are We Heading for Another Housing Collapse?"

11. Kochhar, "Middle Class Fortunes."

12. Goodman and Mayer, "Homeownership and the American Dream."

13. Anderson, *Cowboy Imperialism and Hollywood Film*, 17.

14. Bold, *The Frontier Club*, 40.

15. Davis Hirschfeld, "Trump Calls Some Unauthorized Immigrants."

16. Boyd, *It's Complicated*, 10. "Affordance" is an architectural term for the features of a space that give users access and agency (e.g., door knob, windows, etc.) that has been coopted by digital theorists to describe the tools we use in digital spaces to give us access and agency (e.g., like and sharing buttons).

17. Jenkins, "Game Design," 119, 124.

18. Boyd, *It's Complicated*, 10.

19. Dillon, "A Sea of Texts."

20. I would like to be more specific here, but the game simply deposits stereotypical Indians in this digital space. Fojas, *Border Bandits*, 8.

21. See the gameplay trailers for *Red Dead Redemption* and its prequel—all make claims for historical accuracy.

22. Pease, *The New American Exceptionalism*, 7.

23. Hart, *Empire and Revolution War*, 2.

24. Slotkin, *Gunfighter Nation*, 408.

25. Penix-Tadsen, "Latin American Ludology," 184.

26. Goldberg, *All Your Base Are Belong to Us*.

27. Dittmer, *Popular Culture*, xv.

28. Slotkin, *Gunfighter Nation*, 409–10.

29. Sargeant, "Top Ten Weirdly Racist Video Games." Sargeant at TopTenz writes, "The game caters blatantly to racist stereotypes by building gameplay mechanics that require you to cut-down wave after wave of black and Latino characters, to the point where they lack any semblance of humanity. One level even features a special 'achievement' for killing black people, in a level where your goal is to go into a slum and incite gang warfare."

30. "America's Hispanics."

31. Pease, *The New American Exceptionalism*, 13.

32. LittleBear, "Jagged Worldviews Colliding."

33. Pease, *The New American Exceptionalism*, 13.

34. Aldama, *Latinos and Narrative Media*, 243.

35. Slotkin, *Gunfighter Nation*, 410.

36. Kitses, *Horizons West*, 5, 13.

37. Jagoda, "Fabulously Procedural," 746.

38. Golumbia, "Games without Play," 194.

39. Fojas, *Border Bandits*, 2.

40. Fojas, *Border Bandits*, 2.

41. Fogu, "Digitalizing Historical Consciousness," 103, 121.

42. Rejack, "Toward a Virtual Reenactment," 413.

43. Hart, *Empire and Revolution*, 3.

44. Alonzo, *Badmen, Bandits, and Folk Heroes*, 46, 47.

45. Qtd. in Alonzo, *Badmen, Bandits, and Folk Heroes*, 48.

46. Bhabha, *The Location of Culture*.

47. Hart, *Empire and Revolution*, 3.

48. Mitchell, *Westerns*, 178.

49. See Owen Wister's *The Virginian* for a greater exposition of the proto-neoliberal argument, particularly the four-chapter sequence "The Game and the Nation."

50. Slotkin, *Gunfighter Nation*, 409.

51. Pease, *The New American Exceptionalism*, 8.

52. Landsberg, *Prosthetic Memory*, 21.

53. Moreno, "Why This Mexican-American Designed."

3. VIRTUAL INDIAN REMOVAL

1. Younging, *Elements of Indigenous Style*, 8.
2. Dyer-Witheford and de Peuter, *Games of Empire*, 156.
3. Voorhees, "I Play Therefore I Am," 255. I should note that Gerald Voorhees is specifically talking about the interface of a game titled *Civilization*, which is a turn-based strategy game. However, Voorhees's point that *Civilization* produces an "ego" or an interior self because of the choices the player must make in the game (action and effect) is entirely germane to an action game like *Red Dead Redemption*, which adds another layer to this process of ego formation: embodiment.
4. DiNova, *Spiraling Webs of Relation*, 24.
5. This chapter is primarily informed by indigenist criticism, which recognizes and works to ameliorate social, political, and environmental conditions, even while addressing literary and scholarly concerns. As a white settler scholar with a great deal of cultural privilege, I engage indigenist criticism, but in no way does this critical approach suggest that I possess or understand Indigenous worldviews.
6. Please see Castiglia, *Bound and Determined*, for an excellent analysis of the durability of the female captivity narrative.
7. Miller, "Genre as Social Action."
8. Humphreys, "Oprah's Vigilante Sentimentalism," 214.
9. Slotkin, *Regeneration through Violence*, 5.
10. I use the word "Indian" carefully here. It is a term synonymous with misrepresentation, and so when I use the word "Indian" in this chapter, it is meant to signify that misrepresentation.
11. Bold, "Westerns," 318, 326.
12. Bold, "Westerns," 326.
13. Owens, "White for a Hundred Years," 76, 73.
14. Instead of referencing all Westerns, I'm following Mark Anderson's lead and using the term "frontier western" to denote only those Westerns that embrace the frontier myth, which *Red Dead Redemption* does.
15. Salter and Blodgett, *Toxic Geek Masculinity*, 75.
16. Burrill, "Check Out My Moves," 20.
17. Rifkin, "Settler States of Feeling," 343.
18. Ransom-Wiley, "Activision Issues Apology."
19. Owens, "White for a Hundred Years," 74.
20. Owens, "White for a Hundred Years," 74, 76.

21. Rifkin, "Indigenizing Agamben," 89.

22. Jojola, "Absurd Reality II," 12.

23. Deloria, *Custer Died for Your Sins*, 57.

24. Lamont, "Native American Oral Practice," 379.

25. Rifkin, "Indigenizing Agamben," 89.

26. Davis, *From Homicide to Slavery*, 99.

27. Venables, "The Awesome Mohawk Teacher."

28. Sinclair, "New Ways to Portray Indigenous People."

29. Pettegrew, *Brutes in Suits*.

30. LaPensée qtd. in Sinclair, "New Ways to Portray Indigenous People."

31. Please note that any attempt to remediate an Indigenous story must first be approved by the community and family of the author. This is standard protocol for any settler or any Indigenous person who is not a member of the author's community.

32. Henderson, "Akupachi," 58.

33. Bogost, "The Rhetoric of Video Games," 122.

34. Mourning Dove, *Cogewea*.

35. Mourning Dove, *Cogewea*, 159, 160; Armstrong, "Constructing Indigeneity."

36. Armstrong, "Constructing Indigeneity," 204.

4. "HE'S EVERYTHING"

1. Mitchell, *Westerns*, 156.

2. Bold, *The Frontier Club*.

3. Mitchell, *Westerns*, 156.

4. Wister, *The Virginian*, 3.

5. Salter and Blodgett, *Toxic Geek Masculinity*, 75.

6. Bertozzi, "Marking the Territory," 21.

7. Krutnik, *In a Lonely Street*, 25.

8. Krutnik, *In a Lonely Street*, 204, 93.

9. Salter and Blodgett, *Toxic Geek Masculinity*, 75.

10. Pettegrew, *Brutes in Suits*, 3, 21.

11. Krutnik, *In a Lonely Street*, 93.

12. Jehlen, "The Novel and the American Middle Class," 127.

13. Dilley, "Introduction," 7–8.

14. Berlant, *Cruel Optimism*.

15. Hooks, *Feminist Theory*, 22–23.

16. Voorhees, "Neoliberal Masculinity," 65.

17. Krutnik, *In a Lonely Street*, 93.
18. Kartal, "Liberal and Republican Conceptualizations,"103.
19. Dyer-Witheford and de Peuter, *Games of Empire*, 160.
20. Bold, "Westerns," 318; Voorhees, "Neoliberal Masculinity," 76, my italics.
21. Slotkin, *Gunfighter Nation*, 217, 218.
22. Slotkin, "The Hard-Boiled Detective Story," 92.
23. Krutnik, *In a Lonely Street*, 39.
24. Slotkin, *Gunfighter Nation*, 218.
25. Slotkin, *Gunfighter Nation*, 218.
26. Jack Kelso has several fan sites, one of the more vociferous being the Tumblr "fuckyeahjackkelso," http://fuckyeahjackkelso.tumblr.com/.
27. Users on Reddit comment repeatedly in a thread titled "LA Noire: Jack Kelso—Better than Cole Phelps?" that Kelso is more of a man and hard-boiled detective than Phelps (https://www.reddit.com/r/gaming/comments/hpg9y/la_noire_jack_kelso_better_than_cole_phelps/).
28. Berger and McDougall, "Reading Videogames," 144.
29. Lankoski, "Player Character Engagement," 294.
30. Players learn this fact about the player character while completing side missions before encountering Kalou. These missions build an allegiance between the player and Phelps.
31. Lankoski, "Player Character Engagement," 304.
32. Abbott, *The Street Was Mine*, 10.
33. Salter and Blodgett, *Toxic Geek Masculinity*, 75.
34. Qtd in Slotkin, *Gunfighter Nation*, 218.
35. Ryan, *Avatars of Story*, 99.
36. Pettegrew, *Brutes in Suits*, 199.
37. Broe, *Film Noir, American Workers, and Postwar Hollywood*, 14.
38. Krutnik, *In a Lonely Street*, 93.
39. Jenkins, *Convergence Culture*, 3.
40. Farrow and Iacovides, "Gaming and the Limits of Digital Embodiment," 229.
41. Phelps's failed leadership and his medals for acts of bravery he didn't perform are presented as largely to blame for Sheldon and the other men stealing the army-issue morphine.
42. Krutnik, *In a Lonely Street*, 94–95.

5. BLANCHING NOIRE

1. In this chapter, I'm following Dennis Broe's use of the term "Hollywood noir" in *Film Noir, American Workers, and Postwar Hollywood* to describe

a period of noir. *L.A. Noire* is clearly paying homage to this period. Unlike in chapter 4, where I discuss the construction of masculinity in the game and therefore focus on hard-boiled noir forms, this chapter discusses noir conventions more broadly.

2. Krutnik, *In a Lonely Street*, 209.
3. Broe, *Film Noir, American Workers, and Postwar Hollywood*, 28.
4. Broe, *Film Noir, American Workers, and Postwar Hollywood*, 29.
5. Belsey, "Constructing the Subject," 669–71.
6. Krutnik, *In a Lonely Street*, 202–13.
7. Belsey, "Constructing the Subject," 669.
8. Bogost, *Persuasive Games*, 14.
9. Butler, "Writing on the Body," 402.
10. Farrow and Iacovides, "Gaming and the Limits of Digital Embodiment," 224.
11. Condis, *Gaming Masculinity*, 89.
12. Beck, Boys, and Rose, "Violence against Women," 3025.
13. Beck, Boys, and Rose, "Violence against Women."
14. LeBoeuf, "E3 2019."
15. Hillis, "Film Noir and the American Dream," 1, 2.
16. Copjec, "Introduction," xii.
17. Žižek, *Looking Awry*, 65.
18. Cowie, "Film Noir and Women," 123.
19. Žižek, *Looking Awry*, 65.
20. Rampell, "U.S. Women on the Rise."
21. Salter and Blodgett, *Toxic Geek Masculinity*, 82, 80.
22. Berlant, *The Female Complaint*, 6.
23. Spicer, *Film Noir*, 60.
24. Mulvey, *Visual and Other Pleasures*, 9.
25. Rotskoff, *Love on the Rocks*, 5, 8.
26. Rotskoff, *Love on the Rocks*, 150.
27. Farrimond, "Postfeminist Noir," 35.
28. Landsberg, *Prosthetic Memory*, 2.
29. Landsberg, *Prosthetic Memory*, 2.
30. Broe, *Film Noir, American Workers, and Postwar Hollywood*.
31. Cott, *Public Vows*, 3, 5.
32. Cott, *Public Vows*, 7.
33. Broe, *Film Noir, American Workers, and Postwar Hollywood*, 73.
34. Luxton and Braedley, *Neoliberalism and Everyday Life*, 7.
35. Jenkins, *Convergence Culture*.

36. Luxton and Braedley, *Neoliberalism and Everyday Life*, 8.
37. Abbott, *The Street Was Mine*, 128.
38. Fojas, *Border Bandits*, 2.
39. Berlant, *The Queen of America*, 99.
40. Fojas, *Border Bandits*, 40.
41. Krutnik, *In a Lonely Street*.
42. Berlant, *The Queen of America*, 220.
43. Brown, "Thing Theory," 7.
44. Žižek, *The Sublime Object of Ideology*, 120.
45. Appadurai, *The Social Life of Things*.
46. Sanbonmatsu, "Video Games and Machine Dreams," 474.

6. BURNING DOWN THE HOUSE

1. Giroux, "Disposable Youth in America."
2. Hennelly, "The Middle Class Is Just This Screwed."
3. Gotham, "The Secondary Circuit of Capital Reconsidered," 232.
4. There are so many types of noir in *L.A. Noire* that, for the sake of clarity, I am going to use Frank Krutnik's term "tough thriller" to indicate when I am discussing the type of noir that focuses on masculinity and homosociality. Film noir, as many theorists state, including Krutnik and Dennis Broe, is notoriously difficult to define, but I am solely focused on the genre conventions of tough thrillers and Hollywood noir of the 1940s and into the early 1950s, which are the films and crimes (such as the Black Dahlia murder) that the game references.
5. Osteen, *Nightmare Alley*, 2.
6. Salter and Blodgett, *Toxic Geek Masculinity*, 75.
7. Salter and Blodgett, *Toxic Geek Masculinity*, 75; Krutnik, *In a Lonely Street*, 93.
8. Knobel and Lankshear, "Remix," 23.
9. Broe, *Film Noir, American Workers, and Postwar Hollywood*, xxv.
10. Wilder, *Double Indemnity*; Wyler, *Desperate Hours*.
11. Beuka, *SuburbiaNation*, 5.
12. Landsberg, *Prosthetic Memory*.
13. Broe, *Film Noir, American Workers, and Postwar Hollywood*, xvii.
14. Landsberg, *Prosthetic Memory*, 33.
15. Fogu, "Digitalizing Historical Consciousness," 121.
16. Broe, *Film Noir, American Workers, and Postwar Hollywood*, xxi–xxiv.
17. Himmelstein, *Television Myth and the American Mind*.
18. Smith, "Symbol and Idea in *Virgin Land*," 21–35.

19. Silverblatt, Ferry, and Finan, *Approaches to Media Literacy*, 218.
20. Murphy, *The Suburban Gothic*, 3, 5.
21. Beuka, *SuburbiaNation*, 4.
22. Broe, *Film Noir, American Workers, and Postwar Hollywood*, xxiv.
23. Fay and Nieland, *Film Noir*.
24. Please see the Reddit thread "LA Noire: Jack Kelso—Better than Cole Phelps?" created June 1, 2011, https://www.reddit.com/r/gaming /comments/hpg9y/la_noire_jack_kelso_better_than_cole_phelps/; and the Gamespot forum "Who Else Agrees That Jack Kelso Is . . . *ENDING SPOILERS*," created May 20, 2011, https://gamefaqs.gamespot.com /boards/988983-la-noire/59188692. In some discussions players are upset Phelps dies and angry that Kelso takes over as player character, but more often than not, players liked Kelso over Phelps.
25. Berger and McDougall, "Reading Videogames as (Authorless) Literature," 4.
26. Siodmak, *The Killers*.
27. Broe, *Film Noir, American Workers, and Postwar Hollywood*, 77.
28. Broe, *Film Noir, American Workers, and Postwar Hollywood*, 81.
29. Salter and Blodgett, *Toxic Geek Masculinity*, 75.
30. Mitchell, *Westerns*, 179.
31. Slotkin, *Gunfighter Nation*, 218.
32. Humphreys, "'Truer 'n Hell,'" 38.
33. Hillis, "Film Noir and the American Dream," 10.
34. Osteen, *Nightmare Alley*, 80.
35. Salter and Blodgett, *Toxic Geek Masculinity*, 75.
36. Krutnik, *In a Lonely Street*, 93.

AFTERWORD

1. Stoppard, *Rosencrantz and Guildenstern Are Dead*.
2. I realize the word "genocide" might seem hyperbolic to some, but it isn't. The genocide of Indigenous peoples in North America was attempted through slaughter, residential and industrial schools, germ warfare, and other methods.
3. Burke, *The Philosophy of Literary Form*.
4. Thacker, *Biomedia*, 9.
5. Chess, "The Queer Case of Video Games," 92.

BIBLIOGRAPHY

Abbott, Megan E. *The Street Was Mine: White Masculinity in Hardboiled Fiction and Film Noir*. New York: Palgrave Macmillan, 2002. https://doi.org/10.1057/9781403970015.

Aldama, Frederick Luis. *Latinos and Narrative Media: Participation and Portrayal*. New York: Palgrave Macmillan, 2013.

Alonzo, Juan J. *Badmen, Bandits, and Folk Heroes: The Ambivalence of Mexican American Identity in Literature and Film*. Tucson: University of Arizona Press, 2009.

Anderson, Mark Cronlund. *Cowboy Imperialism and Hollywood Film*. New York: Peter Lang, 2007.

Appadurai, Arjun. *The Social Life of Things: Commodities in Cultural Perspective*. New York: Cambridge University Press, 1986. https://doi.org/10.1017/CBO9780511819582.

Apperley, Thomas H. "Genre and Game Studies: Toward a Critical Approach to Video Game Genres." *Simulation and Gaming* 37, no. 1 (2006): 6–23. https://doi.org/10.1177/1046878105282278.

Armstrong, Jeannette. "Constructing Indigeneity: Syilx Okanagan Oraliture and Tmixwcentrism." PhD dissertation, Universität Greifswald, Greifswald, 2009.

Bakhtin, M. M. *Problems of Dostoevsky's Poetics*. Vol. 8. Edited and translated by Caryl Emerson. Minneapolis: University of Minnesota Press, 1984. https://doi.org/10.5749/j.ctt22727z1.

Bal, Mieke. *Double Exposures: The Practice of Cultural Analysis*. New York: Routledge, 2012. https://doi.org/10.4324/9780203699263.

Beck, Victoria Simpson, Stephanie Boys, Christopher Rose, and Eric Beck. "Violence against Women in Video Games: A Prequel or Sequel to Rape Myth Acceptance?" *Journal of Interpersonal Violence* 27, no. 15 (2012): 3016–31. https://doi.org/10.1177/0886260512441078.

Behrenshausen, Bryan G. "Toward a (Kin)Aesthetic of Video Gaming: The Case of Dance Dance Revolution." *Games and Culture* 2, no. 4 (2007): 335–54. https://doi.org/10.1177/1555412007310810.

Belsey, Catherine. "Constructing the Subject, Deconstructing the Text." In *Feminisms: An Anthology of Literary Theory and Criticism*, edited by Robyn R. Warhol and Diane Price Herndl, 657–73. New Brunswick NJ: Rutgers University Press, 1997.

Bercovitch, Sacvan, and Myra Jehlen, eds. *Ideology and Classic American Literature*. New York: Cambridge University Press, 1987.

Berger, Richard, and Julian McDougall. "Reading Videogames as (Authorless) Literature." *Literacy* 47, no. 3 (2013): 142–49. https://doi.org/10.1111/lit.12004.

Berlant, Lauren, and Jordan Greenwald. "Affect in the End Times: A Conversation with Lauren Berlant." *Qui Parle: Critical Humanities and Social Sciences* 20, no. 2 (2012): 71–89. https://doi.org/10.5250/quiparle.20.2.0071.

Berlant, Lauren Gail. *Cruel Optimism*. Durham NC: Duke University Press, 2011. https://doi.org/10.1215/9780822394716.

———. *The Female Complaint: The Unfinished Business of Sentimentality in American Culture*. Durham NC: Duke University Press, 2008.

———. *The Queen of America Goes to Washington City: Essays on Sex and Citizenship*. Durham NC: Duke University Press, 1997.

Bertozzi, Elena. "Marking the Territory." In *Social Exclusion, Power, and Video Game Play: New Research in Digital Media and Technology*, edited by David G. Embrick, J. Talmadge Wright, and András Lukács, 3–19. Lanham: Lexington, 2012.

Beuka, Robert. *SuburbiaNation: Reading Suburban Landscape in Twentieth-Century American Fiction and Film*. New York: Palgrave Macmillan, 2004. https://doi.org/10.1007/978-1-349-73210-4.

Bhabha, Homi K. *The Location of Culture*. London; New York: Routledge, 1994.

Bogost, Ian. *Persuasive Games: The Expressive Power of Videogames*. Cambridge MA: MIT Press, 2007.

——. "The Rhetoric of Video Games." In *The Ecology of Games: Connecting Youth, Games, and Learning*, edited by Katie Salen, 117-39. Cambridge MA: MIT Press, 2008.

——. *Unit Operations: An Approach to Videogame Criticism*. Cambridge MA: MIT Press, 2006.

Bold, Christine. *The Frontier Club: Popular Westerns and Cultural Power, 1880-1924*. New York: Oxford University Press, 2013.

——. "Westerns." In *The Oxford History of Popular Print Culture*, vol. 6: *US Popular Print Culture, 1860-1920*, edited by Christine Bold and Gary Kelly. Oxford: Oxford University Press, 2012.

Boyd, Danah. *It's Complicated: The Social Lives of Networked Teens*. New Haven: Yale University Press, 2014.

Braedley, Susan, and Meg Luxton. *Neoliberalism and Everyday Life*. Montreal: McGill-Queens University Press, 2014. http://ebookcentral.proquest.com/lib/uvic/detail.action?docID=3332176.

Brisbin, James S. *The Beef Bonanza, or, How to Get Rich on the Plains: Being a Description of Cattle-Growing, Sheep-Farming, Horse-Raising, and Dairying in the West*. Philadelphia: J. B. Lippincott, 1881. http://www.americanwest.amdigital.co.uk/Documents/Details/Case_R_68_.121.

Broe, Dennis. *Film Noir, American Workers, and Postwar Hollywood*. Gainesville: University Press of Florida, 2009.

Brown, Bill. "Thing Theory." *Critical Inquiry* 28, no. 3 (2001): 1-22. https://www.jstor.org/stable/1344258.

Brown, Wendy. "Wounded Attachments." *Political Theory* 21, no. 3 (1993): 390-410. https://doi.org/10.1177/0090591793021003003.

Burke, Kenneth. *The Philosophy of Literary Form: Studies in Symbolic Action*. 3rd ed. Berkeley: University of California Press, 1974.

Burrill, Derek A. "Check Out My Moves." *Social Semiotics* 16, no. 1 (2006): 17-38. https://doi.org/10.1080/10350330500487653.

Butler, Judith. *The Psychic Life of Power: Theories in Subjection*. Stanford: Stanford University Press, 1997.

——. "Writing on the Body: Female Embodiment and Feminist Theory." In *Writing on the Body: Female Embodiment and Feminist Theory*, edited by Katie Conboy, Nadia Medina, and Sarah Stanbury, 401-21. New York: Columbia University Press, 1997.

Castiglia, Christopher. *Bound and Determined: Captivity, Culture-crossing, and White Womanhood from Mary Rowlandson to Patty Hearst*. Chicago: University of Chicago Press, 1996.

Cawelti, John G. *The Six-Gun Mystique*. Bowling Green OH: Bowling Green University Popular Press, 1971.

Cheng, Vincent John. *Inauthentic: The Anxiety over Culture and Identity*. New Brunswick NJ: Rutgers University Press, 2004.

Chess, Shira. "The Queer Case of Video Games: Orgasms, Heteronormativity, and Video Game Narrative." *Critical Studies in Media Communication* 33, no. 1 (2016): 84–94. https://doi.org/10.1080/15295036.2015.1129066.

Clearwater, David. "What Defines a Video Game Genre? Thinking about Genre Study after the Great Divide." *Loading—: The Official Journal of the Canadian Game Studies Association* 5, no. 8 (2011): 29–49.

Condis, Megan. *Gaming Masculinity: Trolls, Fake Geeks, and the Gendered Battle for Online Culture*. Iowa City: University of Iowa Press, 2018.

Copjec, Joan. "Introduction." In *Shades of Noir: A Reader*, edited by Joan Copjec, i-xiii. London: Verso, 1993.

Cowie, Elizabeth. "Film Noir and Women." In *Shades of Noir: A Reader*, edited by Joan Copjec, 121–66. London: Verso, 1993.

Davis, David Brion. *From Homicide to Slavery: Studies in American Culture*. Oxford: Oxford University Press, 1986.

Davis Hirschfeld, Julia. "Trump Calls Some Unauthorized Immigrants 'Animals' in Rant." *New York Times*, May 16, 2018.

Deloria, Vine. *Custer Died for Your Sins: An Indian Manifesto*. New York: Avon, 1969.

Derrida, Jacques. *Acts of Literature*. Edited by Derek Attridge. New York: Routledge, 1992.

Devitt, Amy J. *Writing Genres*. Carbondale: Southern Illinois University Press, 2004.

Dilley, Stephen C. "Introduction." In *Darwinian Evolution and Classical Liberalism: Theories in Tension*. Lanham, UK: Lexington Books, 2013.

Dillon, Elizabeth Maddock. "A Sea of Texts: The Atlantic World, Spatial Mapping, and Equiano's Narrative." In *Religion, Space, and the Atlantic World*, edited by John Corrigan, 25–54. Columbia: University of South Carolina Press, 2017.

DiNova, Joanne. *Spiraling Webs of Relation: Movements toward an Indigenist Criticism*. New York: Routledge, 2019.

Dittmer, Jason. *Popular Culture, Geopolitics, and Identity*. Lanham MD: Rowman and Littlefield, 2010.

Dove, Mourning. *Cogewea, the Half Blood: A Depiction of the Great Montana Cattle Range*. Lincoln: University of Nebraska Press, 1981.

Dyer-Witheford, Nick, and Greig de Peuter. *Games of Empire: Global Capitalism and Video Games*. Minneapolis: University of Minnesota Press, 2009.

Eleteren, Melvan. "Neoliberalization and Transnational Capitalism in the American Mold." *Journal of American Studies* 43, no. 2 (2009): 177–97. https://doi.org/10.1017/s0021875809990016.

Eskelinen, Markku. "The Gaming Situation." *Game Studies: The International Journal of Computer Game Research* 1, no. 1 (2001). http://www.gamestudies.org/0101/eskelinen/.

Farrimond, Katherine. "Postfeminist Noir: Brutality and Retro Aesthetics in the Black Dahlia." *Film and History: An Interdisciplinary Journal* 43, no. 2 (2013): 34–49.

Farrow, Robert, and Ioanna Iacovides. "Gaming and the Limits of Digital Embodiment." *Philosophy and Technology* 27, no. 2 (June 2014): 221–33. https://doi.org/10.1007/s13347-013-0111-1.

Fay, Jennifer, and Justus Nieland. *Film Noir: Hard-Boiled Modernity and the Cultures of Globalization*. London: Routledge, 2009. https://doi.org/10.4324/9780203869680.

Fisher, Mark. *Capitalist Realism: Is There No Alternative?* Hants, UK: O Books, 2009.

Fogu, Claudio. "Digitalizing Historical Consciousness." *History and Theory* 48, no. 2 (May 2009): 103–21. https://doi.org/10.1111/j.1468-2303.2009.00500.x.

Fojas, Camilla. *Border Bandits: Hollywood on the Southern Frontier*. Austin: University of Texas Press, 2008.

Foucault, Michel. "What Is an Author?" In *Language, Counter-Memory, Practice: Selected Essays and Interviews,* edited by Donald F. Bouchard, translated by Donald F. Bouchard and Sherry Simon, 113–38. Ithaca NY: Cornell University Press, 1977.

Freeman, Lance. "America's Affordable Housing Crisis: A Contract Unfulfilled." *American Journal of Public Health* 92, no. 5 (2002): 709–12. https://doi.org/10.2105/AJPH.92.5.709.

Galloway, Alexander R. *Gaming: Essays on Algorithmic Culture*. Minneapolis: University of Minnesota Press, 2006. https://doi.org/10.5749/j.ctttss5p.

Giroux, Henry. "Disposable Youth in America in the Age of Neoliberalism." In *International Encyclopedia of the Social and Behavioral Sciences*, vol. 6, edited by James D. Wright. Amsterdam: Elsevier, 2015.

Goldberg, Harold. *All Your Base Are Belong to Us: How Fifty Years of Videogames Conquered Pop Culture*. New York: Random House, 2011.

Golumbia, David. "Games without Play." *New Literary History: A Journal of Theory and Interpretation* 40, no. 1 (2009): 179.

Goodman, Laurie S, and Christopher Mayer. "Homeownership and the American Dream." *Journal of Economic Perspectives* 32, no. 1 (2018): 31–58. https://doi.org/10.1257/jep.32.1.31.

Gotham, K F. "The Secondary Circuit of Capital Reconsidered: Globalization and the US Real Estate Sector." *American Journal of Sociology* 112, no. 1 (July 2006): 231–75. https://doi.org/10.1086/502695.

Halberstam, Judith. *Female Masculinity*. Durham: Duke University Press, 1998.

Hart, John M. *Empire and Revolution: The Americans in Mexico since the Civil War*. Los Angeles: University of California Press, 2002. https://doi.org/10.1525/j.ctt1pp4v0.

Harvey, David. *A Brief History of Neoliberalism*. New York: Oxford University Press, 2007.

Henderson, James (Sákéj) Youngblood. "Akupachi: Empowering Aboriginal Thought." In *Reclaiming Indigenous Voice and Vision*, edited by Marie Ann Battiste, 248–78. Vancouver: University of British Columbia Press, 2000.

Hennelly, Robert. "The Middle Class Is Just This Screwed: Janet Yellen Declares Victory While the Middle Class Drowns." *Salon*, January 3, 2016. https://www.salon.com/2016/01/03/the_middle_class_is_just_this_screwed_janet_yellen_declares_victory_while_workers_drown/.

Hillis, Ken. "Film Noir and the American Dream: The Dark Side of Enlightenment." *Velvet Light Trap* 55, no. 1 (2005): 3–18.

Himmelstein, Hal. *Television Myth and the American Mind*. New York: Praeger, 1984.

Hooks, Bell. *Feminist Theory: From Margin to Center*. 2nd ed. Cambridge MA: South End Press, 2000.

Howells, Sacha. "Watching a Game, Playing a Movie: When Media Collide." In *ScreenPlay: Cinema/Videogames/Interfaces*, edited by Geoff King and Tanya Krzywinska, 110–21. London: Wallflower, 2002.

Humphreys, Sara. "Oprah's Vigilante Sentimentalism." In *American Exceptionalisms: From Winthrop to Winfrey*, edited by Sylvia Söderlind and James Taylor Carson, 207–22. New York: State University of New York Press, 2011.

———. "'Truer 'n Hell': Lies, Capitalism, and Cultural Imperialism in Owen Wister's *The Virginian*, B. M. Bower's *The Happy Family*, and Mourning Dove's *Cogewea*." *Western American Literature* 45, no. 2 (Spring 2010): 30–52. https://doi.org/10.1353/wal.0.0089.

Jagoda, Patrick. "Fabulously Procedural: Braid, Historical Processing, and the Videogame Sensorium." *American Literature* 85, no. 4 (2013): 745–79. https://doi.org/10.1215/00029831-2367346.

Jehlen, Myra. "The Novel and the American Middle Class." In *Ideology and Classic American Literature*, edited by Sacvan Bercovitch and Myra Jehlen, 125–44. New York: Cambridge University Press, 1986.

Jenkins, Henry. *Convergence Culture: Where Old and New Media Collide*. New York: New York University Press, 2006.

———. "Game Design as Narrative Architecture." In *First Person: New Media as Story, Performance, and Game*, edited by Noah Wardrip-Fruin and Pat Harrigan, 118–30. Cambridge MA: MIT Press, 2003.

Jojola, Ted. "Absurd Reality II: Hollywood Goes to the Indians." In *Hollywood's Indian*, edited by Peter C. Rollins and John E. O'Connor, 12–26. Lexington: University Press of Kentucky, 2010.

Juul, Jesper. *Half-Real: Video Games between Real Rules and Fictional Worlds.* Cambridge MA: MIT Press, 2005.

Kaplan, Amy. "Manifest Domesticity." *American Literature* 70, no. 3 (1998): 581–606. https://doi.org/10.2307/2902710.

Kartal, Filiz. "Liberal and Republican Conceptualizations of Citizenship: A Theoretical Inquiry." *Turkish Public Administration Annual* 27-28 (January 1, 2001).

Keller, Alexandra. "Historical Discourse and American Identity in Westerns since the Reagan Era." In *Hollywood's West: The American Frontier in Film, Television, and History*, edited by Peter C. Rollins and John E. O'Connor, 239–60. Lexington: University Press of Kentucky, 2005.

King, Geoff, and Tanya Krzywinska. *ScreenPlay: Cinema/Videogames/Interfaces.* London: Wallflower, 2002.

King, Thomas. *The Truth about Stories: A Native Narrative.* Toronto: House of Anansi Press, 2003.

Kitses, John. *Horizons West: Anthony Mann, Budd Boetticher, Sam Peckinpah, Studies of Authorship within the Western.* 2nd ed. London: Thames and Hudson, 1970.

Knobel, Michele, and Colin Lankshear. "Remix: The Art and Craft of Endless Hybridization." *Journal of Adolescent and Adult Literacy* 52, no. 1 (2011). https://doi.org/10.1598/JAAL.52.1.3.

Kochhar, Rakesh. "Middle Class Fortunes in Western Europe." Pew Research Center, April 24, 2017. https://www.pewresearch.org/global/2017/04/24/middle-class-fortunes-in-western-europe/.

Kolodny, Annette. *The Land before Her: Fantasy and Experience of the American Frontiers, 1630-1860.* Chapel Hill: University of North Carolina Press, 1984.

Kripke, Pamela. "Are We Heading for Another Housing Collapse?" *New York Post*, September 2, 2017. https://nypost.com/2017/09/02/are-we-headed-for-another-housing-collapse/.

Krutnik, Frank. *In a Lonely Street: Film Noir, Genre, Masculinity.* London: Routledge, 1992. https://doi.org/10.4324/9780203130308.

Kurzweil, Edith. "Review: *Looking Awry: An Introduction to Jacques Lacan through Popular Culture*, by Slavoj Zizek." *American Journal of Sociology* 97, no. 6 (1992): 1786–88. https://doi.org/10.1086/229965.

Lamont, Victoria. "The Bovine Object of Ideology: History, Gender, and the Origins of the 'Classic' Western." *Western American Literature* 35, no. 4 (2001): 373–401. https://doi.org/10.1353/wal.2001.0036.

———. "Native American Oral Practice and the Popular Novel; Or, Why Mourning Dove Wrote a Western." *Western American Literature* 39, no. 4 (2005): 368–93. https://doi.org/10.1353/wal.2005.0007.

Landsberg, Alison. *Prosthetic Memory: The Transformation of American Remembrance in the Age of Mass Culture.* New York: Columbia University Press, 2004.

Lankoski, Petri. "Player Character Engagement in Computer Games." *Games and Culture* 6, no. 4 (June 2011): 291–311. https://doi.org/10.1177/1555412010391088.

LeBoeuf, Sarah. "E3 2019: Only 5% of Games Featured Female Protagonists, down from 8% in 2018 [FemFreq]." *GameDaily.biz*, June 18, 2019. https://gamedaily.biz/article/962/e3-2019-only-5-of-games-featured-female-protagonists-down-from-8-in-2018-femfreq.

LittleBear, Leroy. "Jagged Worldviews Colliding." In *Reclaiming Indigenous Voice and Vision*, edited by Marie Ann Battiste, 77–85. Vancouver: University of British Columbia Press, 2000.

Loxley, James. *Performativity.* New York: Routledge, 2006. https://doi.org/10.4324/9780203391280.

Loyall, Bryan. "Response." In *First Person: New Media as Story, Performance, and Game*, edited by Noah Wardrip-Fruin and Pat Harrigan, 1–33. Cambridge MA: MIT Press, 2003.

Luxton, Meg, and Susan Braedley. *Neoliberalism and Everyday Life.* Montreal: McGill-Queen's University Press, 2010.

May, Elaine Tyler. "Review: *Public Vows: A History of Marriage and the Nation*, by Nancy F. Cott." *Journal of American History* 88, no. 3 (December 2001): 1046–47. https://doi.org/10.2307/2700408.

Miller, Carolyn R. "Genre as Social Action." *Quarterly Journal of Speech* 70, no. 2 (1984): 151–67. https://doi.org/10.1080/00335638409383686.

Mitchell, Lee Clark. *Westerns: Making the Man in Fiction and Film.* Chicago: University of Chicago Press, 1996.

Moos, Dan. *Outside America: Race, Ethnicity, and the Role of the American West in National Belonging.* Hanover: University Press of New England, 2005.

Moreno, Carolina. "Why This Mexican-American Designed a Video Game That Simulates Border Crossings." *Huffington Post*, February 28, 2017. https://www.huffingtonpost.ca/entry/border-crossing-video-game_n_58b5c8f3e4b0780bac2dc22a.

Mulvey, Laura. *Visual and Other Pleasures*. 2nd ed. Bloomington: Indiana University Press, 1989. http://tinyurl.com/y5jhjdnp.

Murphy, Bernice M. *The Suburban Gothic in American Popular Culture*. New York: Palgrave Macmillan, 2009.

Murray, Janet Horowitz. *Hamlet on the Holodeck: The Future of Narrative in Cyberspace*. New York: Free Press, 1997.

Neale, Stephen. *Genre and Hollywood*. London: Routledge, 2000. https://doi .org/10.4324/9780203980781.

Osteen, Mark. *Nightmare Alley: Film Noir and the American Dream*. Baltimore: Johns Hopkins University Press, 2013.

Owens, Louis. "White for a Hundred Years." In *Reading* The Virginian *in the New West*, edited by Melody Graulich and Stephen Tatum, 72–88. Lincoln: University of Nebraska Press, 2003.

Paul, Christopher A. *Wordplay and the Discourse of Video Games: Analyzing Words, Design, and Play*. New York: Routledge, 2012. https://doi.org/10 .4324/9780203124031.

Pease, Donald E. *The New American Exceptionalism*. Minneapolis: University of Minnesota Press, 2009.

Penix-Tadsen, Phillip. "Latin American Ludology: Why We Should Take Video Games Seriously (and When We Shouldn't)." *Latin American Research Review* 48, no. 1 (2013): 174–90. https://doi.org/10.1353/lar.2013.0008.

Pettegrew, John. *Brutes in Suits: Male Sensibility in America, 1890–1920*. Baltimore: Johns Hopkins University Press, 2007.

"A Portrait of America's Middle Class, by the Numbers." NPR, July 7, 2016. https://www.npr.org/2016/07/07/484941939/a-portrait-of-americas -middle-class-by-the-numbers.

Rampell, Catherine. "U.S. Women on the Rise as Family Breadwinner." *New York Times*, May 29, 2013. https://www.nytimes.com/2013/05/30/business /economy/women-as-family-breadwinner-on-the-rise-study-says.html.

Ransom-Wiley, James. "Activision Issues Apology, No Plans to Recall GUN." *Engadget*, February 3, 2006. https://www.engadget.com/2006/02/03 /activision-issues-apology-no-plans-to-recall-gun/.

Rejack, Brian. "Toward a Virtual Reenactment of History: Video Games and the Recreation of the Past." *Rethinking History* 11, no. 3 (2007): 411–25. https://doi.org/10.1080/13642520701353652.

Ricœur, Paul. *A Ricoeur Reader: Reflection and Imagination*. Edited by Mario J Valdés. Toronto: University of Toronto Press, 1991. https://doi.org/10.3138 /9781442664883.

Rifkin, Mark. "Indigenizing Agamben: Rethinking Sovereignty in Light of the 'Peculiar' Status of Native Peoples." *Cultural Critique*, no. 73 (Fall 2009): 88–124. https://doi.org/10.1353/cul.0.0049.

——. "Settler States of Feeling: National Belonging and the Erasure of Native American Presence." In *A Companion to American Literary Studies*, edited by Caroline F. Levander and Robert S. Levine, 342–55. Hoboken NJ: Wiley-Blackwell, 2011. https://doi.org/10.1002/9781444343809.ch21.

Riis, Jacob A. *Theodore Roosevelt, the Citizen.* New York: Macmillan, 1918. http://name.umdl.umich.edu/ACL7419.0001.001.

Ryan, Marie-Laure. *Avatars of Story.* Minneapolis: University of Minnesota Press, 2006. https://doi.org/10.5749/j.ctttv622.

Salter, Anastasia, and Bridget Blodgett. *Toxic Geek Masculinity in Media: Sexism, Trolling, and Identity Policing.* New York: Palgrave Macmillan, 2017. https://doi.org/10.1007/978-3-319-66077-6.

Sanbonmatsu, John. "Video Games and Machine Dreams of Domination." In *Gender, Race, and Class in Media: A Critical Reader*, edited by Gail Dines and Jean M. Humez, 473–83. Los Angeles: SAGE, 2015.

Sargeant, J. F. "Top Ten Weirdly Racist Video Games." *TopTenz*, August 22, 2012. https://www.toptenz.net/top-10-weirdly-racist-video-games.php.

Scharnhorst, Gary. *Owen Wister and the West.* Norman: University of Oklahoma Press, 2015.

Silko, Leslie Marmon. *Ceremony.* New York: Penguin Books, 1988.

Silverblatt, Art, Jane Ferry, and Barbara Finan. *Approaches to Media Literacy: A Handbook.* 2nd ed. London: Routledge, 2001.

Sinclair, Nigaan. "New Ways to Portray Indigenous People in Video Games." *Winnipeg Free Press*, July 16, 2018. https://www.winnipegfreepress.com/opinion/columnists/video-games-488325571.html.

Siodmak, Robert. *The Killers.* NBC Universal, 1946.

Slotkin, Richard. *Gunfighter Nation: The Myth of the Frontier in Twentieth-Century America.* Norman: University of Oklahoma Press, 1998.

——. *The Hard-Boiled Detective Story: From the Open Range to the Mean Streets. The Sleuth and the Scholar: Origins, Evolution, and Current Trends in Detective Fiction.* New York: Greenwood Press, 1988.

——. *Regeneration through Violence: The Mythology of the American Frontier, 1600–1860.* Middletown CT: Wesleyan University Press, 1973.

Smith, Linda Tuhiwai. *Decolonizing Methodologies: Research and Indigenous Peoples.* London; New York: Zed Books, 1999.

"Special Report: America's Hispanics, from Minor to Major." *The Economist*, March 14, 2015. http://www.economist.com/sites/default/files/20150314 _sr_hispanics.pdf.

Spicer, Andrew. *Film Noir*. Harlow: Longman, 2002.

"States with the Highest Foreclosure Rates." CNBC, July 14, 2011. https://www .cnbc.com/2011/07/14/States-With-the-Highest-Foreclosure-Rates.html.

Stoppard, Tom. *Rosencrantz and Guildenstern Are Dead*. London: Faber and Faber, 1968.

Suellentrop, Chris. "Americana at Its Most Felonious." *New York Times*, November 9, 2012. https://www.nytimes.com/2012/11/10/arts/video-games/q -and-a-rockstars-dan-houser-on-grand-theft-auto-v.html.

Tatum, Stephen, and Melody Graulich, eds. *Reading* The Virginian *in the New West*. Lincoln: University of Nebraska Press, 2003.

Thacker, Eugene. *Biomedia*. Minneapolis: University of Minnesota Press, 2004. https://doi.org/10.5749/j.ctttv8m2.

Tompkins, Jane P. *West of Everything: The Inner Life of Westerns*. New York: Oxford University Press, 1992.

Turner, Frederick Jackson. "The Significance of the Frontier in American History." 1893. http://www.f-duban.fr/Sitaduban/Ressources_civ._US /Selected%20texts%20in%20US%20History/TURNER/index.html.

Valverde, Mariana. "Review: *Drinking GenderLove on the Rocks: Men, Women, and Alcohol in Post-World War II America*, by Lori Rotskoff." *Women's Review of Books* 20, no. 4 (January 2003): 19. https://doi.org/10.2307/4024042.

Venables, Michael. "The Awesome Mohawk Teacher and Consultant behind Ratonhnhaké:Ton." *Forbes*, November 25, 2012. https://www.forbes .com/sites/michaelvenables/2012/11/25/the-consultants-behind -ratonhnhaketon/#14ae920d65fe.

Vila, Pablo. *Crossing Borders, Reinforcing Borders: Social Categories, Metaphors, and Narrative Identities on the U.S.-Mexico Frontier*. Austin: University of Texas Press, 2000.

Volkan, Vamik. "Not Letting Go: From Individual Perennial Mourners to Societies with Entitlement Ideologies." In *On Freud's "Mourning Melancholia,"* edited by Thierry Bokanowski, Leticia Glocer Fiorini, and Sergio Lewkowicz, 140–66. London: Karnac Books, 2009.

Voorhees, Gerald. "I Play Therefore I Am: Sid Meier's *Civilization*, Turn-Based Strategy Games and the Cogito." *Games and Culture* 4, no. 3 (2009): 254–75. https://doi.org/10.1177/1555412009339728.

———. "Neoliberal Masculinity." In *Playing to Win: Sports, Video Games, and the Culture of Play*. Bloomington: Indiana University Press, 2015.

West, Cornel. Interview by Anders Stephanson. In *Universal Abandon: The Politics of Postmodernism*, edited by Andrew Ross, 269–86. Minneapolis: University of Minnesota Press, 1988.

Wilder, Billy. *Double Indemnity*. Paramount, 1944.

Wister, Owen. *The Virginian*. New York: Signet Classics, 2002.

Wolf, Mark. "Genre and the Video Game." In *The Medium of the Video Game*, edited by Mark Wolf. Austin: University of Texas Press, 2002.

Wyler, William. *Desperate Hours*. Paramount, 1955.

Yellow Bird, Michael. "What We Want to Be Called: Indigenous Peoples' Perspectives on Racial and Ethnic Identity Labels." *American Indian Quarterly* 23, no. 2 (Spring 1999): 1–21.

Younging, Gregory. *Elements of Indigenous Style: A Guide for Writing by and about Indigenous Peoples*. Edmonton AB: Brush Education, 2018.

Žižek, Slavoj. *Looking Awry: An Introduction to Jacques Lacan through Popular Culture*. Cambridge MA: MIT Press, 1991.

———. *The Sublime Object of Ideology*. London: Verso, 1989.

INDEX

Page numbers in italics refer to illustrations.

in, 135-36; literary conventions in, 6; myth models and, 21, 36; neo-liberalism in, 9, 12, 30-32, 77-78, 89, 122, 128-29; as primary means of storytelling, 11; procedurality of, 1-2; punishment for violating conventions of, 28, 46, 49; remixing genres in, 116-17; socially destructive, 113, 134; stability provided by, 25; storyline flexibility in, 122-23

gangster genre, 77

gay characters, 45-46

gender: and the alcoholic marriage, 98-99, 102-4; evolutionary approach to, 75, 100; games replicating constitution of, 94; noir and, 91-113. *See also* masculinity; white women; women

General Allotment Act, 56

genocide, 60-61, 62, 126, 133-34, 147n2

genre: American identity and, 56-57, 59, 75, 135; analysis, 6, 10-11, 135; classification of, 5; definition of, 4, 57; inequalities built into, 16-17, 33, 55-56, 133, 135; power of, 133, 134; procedural rhetoric and, 13, 134; remixing, 116-17. *See also* durable genres; *specific genres*

Giroux, Henry, 115

Goldberg, Harold, 2, 18, 19, 42

Gold Rush, 16

Golumbia, David, 28-29, 46

Gotham, Kevin, 115-16

Grand Theft Auto (game series), 2, 121

Grand Theft Auto: Vice City, 77-78

Graulich, Melody, 7

Great Plains, 41, 52, 60-61

Great Recession, 11, 22, 24, 38;

depoliticization of, 24-25; female breadwinners and, 96; home foreclosures resulting from, 24, 38, 115-16; resignation to, 128-29; "security" and, 104-5

Grinnell, George Bird, 7, 17, 58

Grusin, Richard, 6

GUN, 60-61

Gunfighter Nation (Slotkin), 78

Gunslinger, 38

Halberstam, Jack, 139n8

The Happy Family (Bower), 37

hard-boiled detective: and the American Dream, 95, 116; characteristics of, 126-27; and frontier myth, 8, 75-78, 83; "little man" protected by, 127; vs. police detective, 79-80, 83-87, 88-89, 126-27; purpose of, 78-79; Raymond Chandler defining, 83-84

Hart, John Mason, 41

Harvey, David, 30

Hawkeye (Natty Bumppo), 57, 78, 84, 88, 128

Hearst, William Randolph, 48-49

hegemonic masculinity, 78

Henry, Celine (character), 97, 98, 100-105, *101*, 108, 111

Henry, Jacob (character), 101, 102-3, 104, 105

Henry, Judge (character), 9

Hillis, Ken, 95

Himmelstein, Hal, 120

history: erasing, 59; gameplay as, 47; historicity and, in *L.A. Noire*, 99-100, 119-20; historicity and, in *Red Dead Redemption*, 18, 41, 42, 47-48, 50-51, 55-56, 140n21; spatializing, 119-20

misogyny, 74–75, 92, 96–113
Mitchell, Lee Clark, 17, 22, 28; on convalescence in Westerns, 30; on the cowboy's body, 73
Moller, Diedre (character), 110, 111, 112
Moller, Hugo (character), 112
Monroe, Leland (character), 126, 127, 128, 129, 130
mourning, perpetual state of, 23–24
Mourning Dove, 13, 68–71
Mulvey, Laura, 97
Murray, Janet, 18, 110
mythic symbols, 41
myth models, 21

narrative norms, resistance to, 84–85
narratives and lived experience, 21
narratology vs. ludology debate, 4
Nastas (character), 63, *63*, 64–65
naturalism, 10
Neale, Steve, 3
neocolonialism, 11, 12
neoliberalism, 9–10, 12, 19, 76; Bonnie MacFarlane representing, 26; definition of, 19; and depoliticization of suffering, 31; and frontier myth, 21, 30, 77–78; futility of resisting, 122; in game worlds, 9, 12, 30–32, 77–78, 89, 122, 128–29; vs. liberalism, 76–77; masculinity and, 77, 85, 89; opting out of, 30–31; performing, 30; resignation to, 128–29; resistance to, 27; vs. socialism, 106, 107–8; in *The Virginian*, 141n49
"Neoliberal Masculinity" (Voorhees), 78
New Austin, 11, 21–22, 27; geography of, 39–41, *39*

Nieland, Justice, 3
nihilism, 121–22, 130
9/11 attacks, 24
"Noble Native/Savage Indian" dichotomy, 58
noir (genre), 2–3, 113; gender roles in, 91–113; genre conventions disrupted by, 3; hard-boiled, 3, 6, 12–13, 78; hero of, 74, 79–80; iconography of, 6; instability in, 104–5, 117, 118; McCarthy-era, 125; "social problem" media in, 91, 98; veterans in, 129–30; and Western, relationship between, 3, 8–9; whiteness in, 82; working women punished in, 95–96
Nuevo Paraiso, 11, 22, 35–53; as "below" New Austin, *39*, 40, 41; missions set in, 44–53, 140n3

Osteen, Mark, 129–30
Ottie, Merlon (character), 82, *82*
Outlaw, 5
"over-civilization," weakness caused by, 37
Owens, Louis, 61, 135

patriotism, 27
Paul, Christopher, 111
Pease, Donald, 43–44
Pendix-Tadsen, Philip, 41
performativity, 21, 29–30, 36, 52–53, 55–56, 142n3
persecution, fantasy of, 9
Petersen, Leonard (character), 121, 127–28
Pettegrew, John, 75, 77, 85, 89
The Phantom Lady (Woolrich), 92

CPSIA information can be obtained
at www.ICGtesting.com
Printed in the USA
LVHW090705210221
679533LV00014B/1038